A
Wandering
of
Gypsies

The autobiography of two present-day Romanies

Tom and Julie McCready

Publisher: Robert Dawson, Blackwell, Derbyshire, 2001.

A WANDERING OF GYPSIES

Text and photographs copyright Tom and Julie McCready

First Published in 2001 by
Robert Dawson
188 Alfreton Road,
Blackwell,
Alfreton,
Derbys.
DE55 5JH

ISBN 1-903418-10-0

Printed by 4 Sheets Design & Print Ltd, 197 Mansfield Road, Nottingham NG1 3FS

Foreword

by Jenny Boyd-Cropley of Cottage Books

Biographies, let alone autobiographies of authentic Travellers in Britain, have rarely been published. The few which have found their way into print have been instantly popular with all who have any interest in Gypsies and their way of life and once such books are out of print, demand for them always outstrips the supply.

Therefore it was with some excitement and great anticipation that I received the manuscript of *A Wandering of Gypsies* by Tom and Julie McCready to read through, and I was far from disappointed.

This is a very readable, detailed and thoroughly enjoyable autobiography of two English Travellers, recalling their childhood and young adulthood growing up in the 1940s and 50s - Tom was born in 1936 and Julie in 1940. The first part of the book is Tom's story, which is followed by Julie's. Both give a first hand account of life during World War II and during the period of austerity which followed, a clear insight into the daily lives of young Travelling people, their families and the way of life of their community. There is also a great deal of family history and background detail of the lives of their extended families.

The book finishes with their marriage while both were still in their teens, starting their lives together in a tent. That was over 40 years ago, and although they have recently settled on a privately owned site in South Yorkshire, most of their married life has been spent Travelling in the East Midlands and South Yorkshire; they have raised five children, all of whom have married into Traveller families and have numerous grandchildren, all of whom have grown up to also marry Travellers..

Tom and Julie have always followed the traditional way of life and until ill health intervened, Tom was still busy doing grinding and Julie hawking with a tushni of lace and lucky charms as well as doing a bit of dukkering.

Both Tom and Julie are very respected members of the Traveller community and I am greatly honoured that they have asked me to write the foreword for their book. I am sure all who read it will agree that this authentic account of Traveller life in the mid 20th Century portraying not a rosy romantic picture of imagination, but a genuine record of the hardships, trials and deprivation and hard work even young people were expected to endure, as well as the freedom, enjoyment and satisfaction of life in the close and caring Traveller community, is a welcome addition to our knowledge of a way of life now all but disappeared and I hope that like me you will fid that this honest, enthusiastic and affectionate account of the authors' younger days is a book that, once you have started reading, you are unable to put it down ...

Jenny Boyd-Cropley, Cottage Books

TOM'S STORY

Tom's Story

My earliest memories are of a house in Stockport. Hopwoods Court, Heaton Norris as I recall. Not the usual first memories for a Gypsy, but then they were unusual times, 'Don't you know there's a war on?' was the catch phrase of the day. Believe me, we knew.

Dad was in the army and the vardo (horse drawn caravan) I'd lived in since my birth in Stepping Hill Hospital had been sold, along with horses and harness. Apparently it was felt that being on the road with a small child was too much to expect my mother to cope with.

Many of Mother's sisters had the same idea and had all settled in Stockport. Aunt Lina had a house in Hesketh Street, Aunt Lizzie a house in Short Street, Aunt Francis in Portwood and Aunt Helen in Hillgate.

Hopwoods Court was a small terrace of about ten houses in an unpaved street - there was a pavement but the road itself was just hard packed earth. Barrage balloons dotted the sky and a huge water tank with the letters EWS (emegency water supply) painted on made an ideal model boat pond.

Before I was old enough to attend school, I was usually left with one or other of the aunts during the day whilst Mother went hawking. On occasion she would take me with her and I remember catching the early morning tram or 'bus to various areas around Stockport. I can remember much of her spiel today.

"Are you buying me up today lady?" She would begin. Then without stopping long enough for the woman to reply, would continue. "Don't turn your luck away, you've a lucky face to say 'not today'. I can see you've had your ups and downs and up to now it hasn't all been straight, but there's better things in store. Remember, a still tongue makes a wise head but never let your left hand know what your right hand's going to do. Buy a little something from a lucky Gypsy lady and let me tell you some thing you want to know."

The basket of small-ware would be displayed: buttons, iodine, wintergreen, smelling salts, combs, toothpaste, and elastic etc. Often the woman would buy some small item just to get rid of Mother, but sometimes she would be invited in to tell the lady's fortune. I looked forward to these occasions for I would often be given a drink of pop or a bit of cake whilst they talked.

Air raids were exciting. We had an Anderson Shelter in the back yard but Mother didn't trust it. At the first wail of the siren she would throw me in a 'pram and set off at break-neck speed for the shelter down Rock Hill. This shelter was carved out of solid rock and went on for hundreds of feet through the hill, the other entrance being on Dodge Hill.

Rock Hill was very steep and Mother seemed to take twelve foot strides, with sparks coming from her clogs as she hung on to the 'pram in the dash for safety. Being only four foot ten, she must have been a comical sight. I remember one old man saying to her, as we screeched to a halt outside the shelter entrance.

"Ee lass, I thought tha' were a runaway 'oss when I 'eard tha' comin'."

2

Perhaps this would be as good a time as any to introduce the reader to my parents and their families, or at least tell what I know of them.

My father was from the Potteries where most of his family had settled some years before. All I know of his parents is that they were called Tom and Julie. Dad had two brothers, Tom and Cecil; his sisters were Maggie, Julie and Janet.

Maggie lived in Halmer End, near Alsager in the Potteries. Her husband was Ben Hulse and they had a daughter Margaret. There was a son, Sam, by Ben's first marriage, Ben's first wife having died young.

Julie I know almost nothing of, except she was wealthy, lived in Birmingham and had little to do with the rest of the family.

Janet kept a little sweet shop in Halmer End. On the one occasion I called in she made it clear by her attitude that I wasn't welcome, ushering me out of the shop as soon as I'd made my purchase. I saw her husband once but never knew his name.

Tom lived in Wood Lane, a village not far from Halmer End. His son was in the army and during a visit with my parents Tom's wife offered to give me her son's old meccano set, much to my delight. Uncle Tom however vetoed the idea and as a child I never forgave him.

Cecil was a regular soldier and an officer - I don't know his rank. He was a prisoner of the Japanese in Singapore but survived to re-enlist.

Mother was the daughter of Levi Vitus and Elizabeth Finney. Old Vitus's Mother was a Miller. Granny Lizzie was a Varey before she married. Their children, in order of age, eldest first were: Martha, Ellen, Tom, Annie, (my Mother) Francis, Lizzie, Billy, Lina and Louisa.

Martha was the only one I didn't know. She died of gangrene giving birth to her second child, the baby being stillborn. She had married Isaac Rowles and they had a daughter, Ellen. I was a babe in arms at the time of Martha's death. Isaac used to call at our house from time to time and bring Ellen, who was my age to play with me.

Aunt Ellen's marriage was to Peter Winter. She was a big woman physically with a personality to match and they had three children: Jimmy, Martha and Annie.

Uncle Tom married a gaujo (non Gypsy) girl who bore him around fifteen children. Those I can recall are: Vitus, Jimmy, Johnny, David, Charlie, Peter, Billy, Freddie, Kathleen, Ellen, Martha, Rita and Francis.

Mother married Sam McCready and apart from a brief period during the war, they lived life the Romani way. They had a daughter, stillborn, in a waggon at Hazel Grove, Stockport. Dad made the coffin and carried it in his arms to bury her in the local cemetery. This would be the reason Mother went into Stepping Hill Hospital to have me, five years later in 1936.

Typical of the poverty of the time was the story Dad told me of the grindstone he made. In need of a grindstone to go door-to-door, sharpening household goods, and not having funds to by a stone, he decided to make one. Cut from a paving stone with a hammer and chisel; perfectly round and with a hole in the centre to take the spindle, it took three days to make. Dad said it was a great success and he used it for many years.

Francis and her husband, Jim Varey had two children, Lizzie and Charlie.

Billy married a Stockport lass and at the outbreak of war, fled to Ireland, leaving her with several children. In Dublin he bigamously married an Irish girl and had children by her. The law caught up with him, however, and he served eighteen months in Mountjoy Prison.

Lina comes next. Her husband was known as Sam Lock, but Sam's father was brother to my wife's grandfather, Silvester (Trout) Taylor. Sam probably took his grandmother's name, a common enough practice among Gypsies.

Louisa, or Louie as she was called, married Jack Varey and had three sons: Johnny, Billy and Jimmy. Their only daughter was called Eva. More of these families later.

Both my parents were illiterate. Mother, however, knew the alphabet and taught it me by writing it in chalk on the back of an old horsehair sofa we had. This got me off to a good start when I enrolled as a pupil at Christ Church Infants School, just before my fifth birthday. Three months or so at school saw me reading well enough to read the letters Dad sent home to Mother. An army pal wrote these for him.

As a reward for doing so well at school, Dad brought me my first book when he came on leave. 'Saved by a Bear' was a thick volume of children's stories and I treasured it.

On my way to school one day I found two bombs, just lying on the ground by the park railings. I took off in great terror, running straight into the arms of the local policeman who was quick to grab me and stop my headlong flight.

"Now then, now then lad, what's up?" he asked. Holding tight to my wrist.

"It's a bomb!" I shouted, trying to break away. "It's a bomb!"

"Steady on son," the policeman said, tightening his grip. "A bomb? You'd better show me."

Reluctantly I took him back to the park and showed him my find. To my amazement he started to laugh.

"They're not bombs son," he chuckled. "They're gas cylinders. The workmen are going to cut down the park railings today for scrap iron. We'll make bombs out of the iron to drop on Hitler."

Still not really convinced, I gave the cylinders a wide birth as I continued my journey to school.

Everyone at this time had a gas mask. I carried mine to and from school in the little cardboard box provided with it. All the children at school had regular drills when we would don our masks and run around the school playground. Woe betide any child arriving at school without his gas mask - it was drilled into us that it must be carried at all times.

Gas masks came in three different styles, or at least I remember three types. Standard masks were provided for all adults and children down to about pre-school age. Younger children had a 'Mickey Mouse' mask with a long, floppy red nose and two ears, supposedly to make it less frightening to the little ones. I couldn't see the logic of this myself, the small child wearing it couldn't see it but could see the ugly masks everyone else was wearing. Infants were provided with a big dome shaped mask, very much like a huge diver's helmet. Baby was placed inside this contraption and someone had to operate a little set of bellows to pump air to the child.

Other happier memories that come to me include: Collecting a pillow case full of hazel nuts in Vernon Park one hot summer's day when Dad was on leave. Trying to catch pigeons by putting salt on their tails, (The policeman gave me this tip.) And visiting various relatives in their waggons and tents with my mother.

Some of the stopping places had names like: Fisher's Fields, Ashton Moss, Windy Harbour and Dark Lane.

One memory that stands out, perhaps because I got a jigsaw puzzle out of it, was that of a young man who lived a couple of doors away. On the eve of his departure to join the unit to which he had been posted he stood at his bedroom window throwing his books and toys down to a gang of children waiting below. Mother told me he was off to fight Hitler next day and I thought him very brave.

Aunt Lina had broken her leg and the 'pot' had been on a few weeks. When we arrived at her house one morning she said to Mother.

"Our Annie, this plaster shouldn't come off for another couple of weeks, but my leg's better now and I'm sick to death of dragging it around. Do you think me and you could get it off? It'd save me 'avin to go to the 'ospital."

"If your sure it's mended," said Mother. "We'll soon 'ave it off. We'll need some 'ot water though. Put the kettle on Lina."

It took the best part of the morning, several kettles of hot water, a bread knife, a small hacksaw, various spoons and a hammer. The house was a shambles, plaster and water seemed to get everywhere-but they did it. Levering off the last piece of plaster, Lina smiled triumphantly and stood up. Or rather she tried to stand. As soon as her foot touched the floor, she screamed in pain and collapsed in a heap on the floor.

"Oh! it's agony," she sobbed. "I can't bear to put my weight on it, the pain's terrible, it must be still broke. Whatever shall we do?"

"You'll 'ave to go to 'ospital again," Mother said, helping Lina into a chair.

"Ow are we going to get there?" Lina asked. "I couldn't get to the 'bus stop like this."

It would never have occurred to either of them to ring for an ambulance and funds didn't run to a taxi.

"I'll take you in the 'pram," Mother decided.

"What are we going to tell them?" Lina asked, tearfully. "They'll go mad when they know we've took it off."

"We'll think of something." Mother replied. "Come on, it'll 'ave to be seen to. Get in the 'pram I'll get you there."

"How did it come off?" a nurse asked at the hospital.

"I fell down the cellar steps and it just broke." said Lina. Mother nodded in agreement.

"Come of it," the nurse laughed. "I bet it took you ages to get that off, didn't it?"

"I thought it was better," replied a shamefaced Lina. "I'm sorry."

"Yes, I bet you are," smiled the nurse, wheeling Lina off to the plaster room. "Perhaps you'll let us take it off next time?"

"Oh I will, I will! I won't touch it again don't you worry about that." replied an embarrassed Lina.

Aged about six, I was allowed to go on my own to see a Tarzan film in town. There was a huge stuffed lion in the foyer and for the life of me I couldn't bring myself to walk past it, it seemed so lifelike. After several abortive attempts I went to see a

George Formby film instead. When I think of it now, I'm surprised I was allowed to go into town alone at that age, but then, they were different times.

My playmates then were cousins Charlie and Lizzie. Charlie was two years younger than I, and Lizzie a little older. Also, as I've mentioned, Cousin Ellen was a regular visitor.

The houses in Hopwoods Court were plagued with bed bugs and Mother fought a constant battle with them. She'd strip off wallpaper and whitewash the walls, lever off skirting boards and paint behind them with paraffin before sealing the rooms one by one and burning sulphur candles in them. Such treatment had to be carried out surreptitiously for if the next-door neighbours found out what was being done, they would complain that you were driving the bugs from your house into theirs. Nothing seemed to work for long however - the bugs always came back.

Acquiring a new flock bed from somewhere, Mother decided to get rid of the old one by dumping it on some land several streets away known locally as the 'rec. We rolled it up as best we could and tied it on our only means of transport - a 'pram with a squeaky wheel. Late at night, we set off through the unlit streets and across the 'rec.

Reaching our chosen spot, Mother cut the string holding the bed and tipped it down a grassy bank. The night was coal black and we just didn't see the courting couple in the grass below. We heard their shouts of alarm, however, as the bed landed on top of them. Grabbing me with one arm, Mother threw me into the 'pram and made for home at great speed with the 'pram wheel squeaking like a demented budgie. I often smile when I think of the surprise the couple must have felt when a bed arrived, seemingly from nowhere.

Loud knocking at the door woke us late one night.

"Who ever's that?" said Mother. "It's past midnight. There must be summat up." And she hurried downstairs to find out. I trailed behind as she opened the front door. It was Dad.

"What's wrong Sam? What's the ever's matter? Have you gone AWOL? (Absent with out leave) asked Mother, pulling Dad inside. Father had gone AWOL once before and had been caught hiding under the mattress in Aunt Lina's waggon on Fisher's Fields, with Aunt Lina in bed on top of him. He'd served time in the glasshouse for that.

Dad was beaming all over his face.

"No, It's nowt like that love," he grinned. "I'm out, they've chucked me out of the army."

"Why? What 'ave you done?" Mother asked, filling the kettle for tea.

"I've done nowt," said Dad. "Here son, read that for your mam before she worries herself to death."

Taking the paper Dad waved at me I read something along the lines of 'Discharged for work of national importance.'

"What is it Dad?" I asked. I had visions of him being engaged in some special work, a spy perhaps or a secret agent.

"It's working in a brick yard at Chesterton in the Potteries," he explained. "I went to see about it on my last leave, when I visited my sister Maggie. The manager said he'd see what he could do but I didn't mention it 'cos I didn't think anything would come of it. It means we'll have to move."

"I won't be sorry to see the back of this place," Mother said, kissing him. "We'll get a waggon and pull in Hancock's Yard."

"There's no time for that," said Dad. "I start work in five days. I'll have to go and stay at our Maggie's 'till we can get something sorted."

Dad went off to his sister's at the weekend. Mother and I followed a week or two later by furniture van. Maggie had offered us the use of her front room on a temporary basis.

Staying at Halmer End was not a happy experience. I was bullied at school, being the only Gypsy child there. Luckily, one of the teachers, on discovering this, arranged for me to be let out of school fifteen minutes before the rest of the kids were turned loose. This arrangement suited me fine.

My parents had some money stolen from a drawer in the room that had been allocated to us. We never found the culprit but suspicion fell on one of Dad's relatives, a work-shy young man who shall be nameless.

This encouraged my parents to redouble their efforts to find a waggon. Mother was sent to the post office to send a telegram to Aunt Lina, who by this time was stopping in Fisher's Fields.

Dictating the telegram to the postmistress, she began:

"Dear Lina hoping this letter finds you all well as it leaves us the same here at present...." Only to be interrupted by the postmistress who explained that telegrams cost so much a word. Duly shortened, the message was sent.

A reply came by letter a couple of days later, saying that Saky Finney had a waggon for sale and giving relevant details. Dad caught the train to Manchester after work that night and the purchase was completed.

Sam Lock, Lina's husband offered to take the waggon as far as Stockport and a local farmer and his horse was hired to meet him there and bring it the rest of the way to Hancock's Yard. In the event, the farmer packed the job in at Talk Pits, some three miles or so from his destination, saying it was too much for his horse and abandoning the waggon in the gateway to a field.

That night, various friends and relatives were rounded up and an attempt made to pull the waggon the rest of the way by people power. The first hill they met was the long pull from Talk Pits to Red Street and it proved too long and steep for them. Although they pushed, swore and sweated for more than an hour they made little progress and had to admit defeat.

"Leave it," said Dad. "We'll see if we can't change the farmer's mind in the morning." With that the waggon was pushed onto the grass verge and left again.

Dad being at work, Mother went to see the farmer next day. Eventually he agreed to finish the job, explaining that the throat band on the horse's bridle was just a bit of rope and that it had tightened in the rain, restricting the horse's air supply. He'd discovered the problem he said, when he'd come to un-harness the horse back in the stable. The fact that he hadn't been paid probably influenced his decision to see the job through and that day the waggon was finally delivered to Hancock's.

Within a few days, the few sticks of furniture we had were sold and we moved from Halmer End. Hancock's was a much happier place to live, for me at least. Other boys my age there included Jimmy Douglas, Victor Lee and Albert Hancock.

Jimmy was the only son of a Gypsy family living on the site. Victor's father had married the owner's daughter, and Albert, a gaujo, was the owner's grandson.

Victor was my age; he was a good-looking lad, a James Mason look-alike. His dad collected scrap with a horse and cart. Victor and I would sometimes spend a Saturday helping on the round in return for picture money.

Albert was a thickset boy with close-cropped blond hair. He and I had several fights over the years. Albert usually won; he was too good for me. The only two occasions that I beat him were when he was enraged and came at me like a mad bull. The fights when he threw caution to the wind I managed to win. When he fought coolly and calmly, I had no chance. After each fight we would shake hands and be the best of friends, 'till the next time.

Jimmy Douglas lived with his parents in a trailer - the first Gypsies I'd seen with one. His dad owned a big straight eight Buick and I longed for a ride in it. Jimmy never seemed short of money. He always had a couple of pound notes tucked into a little pocket in the front of his trousers. Times when we kids were all skint, which were fairly frequent, Jim would often treat us all to a night at the pictures.

One Sunday, several of the kids at Hancock's planned a 'bike ride to Crewe, some eight miles or so away. Albert said he would come with us.

"How can you come?" Victor asked. You haven't got a 'bike.

"I'll run there," said Albert. "It's only about eight miles. No problem."

"You can't run eight miles," I said. "Besides, you'll have to run back as well, you can't do it."

"Want to bet?" said Albert.

"Yes, a shilling on it. But you're not riding with me if you get tired," I replied.

"You're on, an' I don't want to ride with any of yus," Albert retorted. I can do it easily."

All attempts to dissuade him proved futile, so we set off with Albert trotting along beside us. I was confident that Albert couldn't do it and thought he would give up after the first mile or so. When after five miles, Albert was still with us, drenched in sweat but plodding doggedly on, I wasn't so sure.

"Come on, get on the crossbar," I told Albert. "You'll make yourself bad."

"I'm not paying you a shilling," he said. "I 'av'n't got one."

"Neither have I," I admitted. "Come on, let's forget it."

"Ok," smiled Albert. "But you ride on the crossbar and I'll pedal, you must be tired."

About a mile from Hancock's was Red Street, where a Sybil Teaton also had a site for Gypsies. Sybil didn't have a tractor on her small farm and used a Rolls Royce car with the body chopped off as a substitute. With a wooden platform fitted, it made a useful vehicle for all her farm work.

My maternal grandparents, Grandad Vitus Finney and Grannie Lizzie, were stopping on this camp at this time. Uncle Tom Finney, (Mother's brother,) one of the Toogoods and a Varey family were amongst the other residents.

Many of the children from both camps attended the local school - Albert Street Junior Boys. Although the Gypsy element at this school fluctuated as families came and went, there was always enough of us to hold our own in the school playground.

Consequently, that was an end to any bullying problems.

There was no main water on Hancock's, not even in the owner's house, Rose Cottage. All water had to be carried from the single tap that served a row of about ten houses roughly a mile away. This was a daily chore I hated, as I suppose did the rest of the community. Nonetheless, for this privilege, we received a regular water rate demand.

Another job I disliked was picking coal on the old pit tip not far away. Scratching about with dead fingers on a frosty morning for a few nuggets of coal was very cold work indeed. Carrying the coal the half mile or so home, soon warmed you up however.

Before I give the wrong impression let me hasten to add that this part of my life, though hard, was an extremely happy time.

Over the next couple of years or so, other members of my extended family moved onto the site. These included Uncle Sam Lock and Aunt Lina, with their son Peter, two years younger than I, and younger daughter Louisa. Sam had just been discharged from his regiment - The Lancashire Fusiliers. Uncle Jim Varey, also newly discharged from the army, moved on with his wife Francis, daughter Lizzie and son Charlie.

People came and went all the time, as did we once the war was over and Dad could leave his job.

V.E. day saw us at Hancock's. Some of the gaujos living nearby organised a huge party and went round the caravan site to invite every Gypsy child to attend. The party was held on the huge lawn of a local farm and I went with Peter and Charlie.

When he saw the several tables laden with food, Peter's eyes widened.

"Have I got to eat all that?" He asked, in astonishment - much to the amusement of the gaujos present.

We were at Hancock's for the winter of forty-seven, for I remember the big snow. So deep was it that we dug a stable for the horses out of a drift and with a bit of straw on the ground, they were quite comfortably.

Aunt Lina gave birth to her daughter Ann during this winter for I remember seeing blood in the snow outside their waggon.

There was a short steep hill called Chain Bank on Audley Road, just before Rose Cottage. During the snow, a gang of us kids spent one early morning polishing the road to a glass like finish. Then we waited for cars to come along and get stuck climbing the hill. Our offer to help push them up for a shilling (five pence) was always accepted. Cars weren't as frequent then as now but in the morning we earned twelve shillings and were suddenly rich. About midday a tractor and trailer came and gritted the road, putting an end to our little enterprise.

When we kids were in funds it was often spent on a trip to the local cinema, or 'Maggie Shemult's Bug Hut' as it was known locally. Roy Rogers and Trigger, Zorro, Flash Gorden, Tarzan, King Kong, The Three Stooges and others of that ilk were our steady diet.

The cheapest seats cost a threepenny bit, (one and a half new pence) and when Eric Shemult had got us all in our seats; with many a painful dig in the ribs from his torch, he would come around and spray us all with a fine mist.

For our shilling, we could get a night at the pictures, an ice cream, a bag of chips and 'bus fare home.

Shemult must be a German name and although I didn't think of it at the time, I've since wondered what life must have been like for them in war time England.

Other ways of earning pocket money included taking empty milk bottles back to the shop for a shilling a dozen, fetching water for other resident and doing any other odd jobs we were offered.

In season I picked potatoes, helped get the hay in and on one occasion helped hoe a seemingly endless field of some crop or other. This work was done after school or at weekends. Many of the local farmers made use of our services from time to time. To the best of my knowledge my parents never gave me pocket money. Times were hard, they worked hard and I just didn't expect any.

Summer was the time to travel, but sometimes, for reasons of illness or such we were compelled to spend some weeks of the summer at Hancock's. This was our base where we could be sure of stopping whilst we got our problems sorted.

One glorious summer day there, the Gypsy kids organised an 'Olympic Games' as we called it. Broken toys and old comics were the prizes and we made wooden elder flowers to give away as rosettes. Local gaujo children were invited to compete and some of them donated prizes.

Competitions included the usual running races, long and high jumps, a football match - Jimmy having bought a proper ball - a cricket match, a swimming contest - four times across Packers Pool - and a singing contest.

Starting about noon, the games went on 'till late in the evening. Gypsy families on the camp provided us with several lots of sandwiches and a good time was had by all.

Janice, a gaujo girl from the row of houses where the tap was situated took the lion's share of prizes, including the singing contest. We all vowed to do it again at some time, but we never did.

About the time war came to an end, Dad begged me a puppy. He was very small when he arrived and could barely lap. Jet black, he grew to be a massive animal. I think he was an Alsation-Labrador cross. I called him Nigger (that wouldn't do today but the name had no racial connotations for me at the time) and he was a boy's best friend. We went everywhere together. Coming home from school I would find him in lying in the grass beside the road waiting for me. We explored the woods, he'd be with me when I picked coal, swam in Packer's pool or fetched water. In fact if at all possible, where I was, he was.

When bonfire night came around we would cut bushes down and drag them back to the bonfire. Nigger did his share, dragging a bush tied to his collar. He was immensely strong and could pull with the best of us, seemingly enjoying every minute of it.

Dad bought me two baby ducks from Newcastle cattle market. Uncle Jim, Charlie's dad bought one for Charlie. We kept them together in an improvised wire -mesh pen. One morning two of them had disappeared and search as we might we couldn't find them.

"I bet that dog of yours 'as eaten 'em," said Charlie.

"Nar, don't be daft," I replied. "Nigger wouldn't do a thing like that. Let's 'ave another look round the ground, they must be somewhere."

After another fruitless search we returned to stare ruefully at the remaining duckling.

10

"Say what you like," Charlie said. I'd swear that jukle (dog) of yours 'as 'ad 'em."

"Never," I leaped to Nigger's defence. "He wouldn't. I'll tell you what to do, you put the duck near Nigger an' I'll 'old his collar 'an we'll see what he does."

"Right," Charlie said, catching up the remaining duckling. "'Old that dog tight now."

Charlie placed the duck on the ground near Nigger who made a terrific lung forward, pulling me off my feet. With one gulp he swallowed the duckling whole and sat there thumping his tail with delight at the unexpected treat. At least we'd solved the mystery of the missing ducklings.

Nigger was an inveterate thief, and this was to be his downfall. Bacon joints, shoes, loaves of bread, children's toys, other dog's dinners, it was all the same to him. Once he came home carrying a pan of boiling hot potatoes by the handle, obviously just removed from someone's gas stove. Later it was discovered that he had taken them from a neighbouring house when the house owner had left the kitchen door open to allow the steam to escape. Next day Nigger had vanished. I searched everywhere for him, walking miles calling his name. No Nigger.

"Shut up moaning about that dinglo (daft) jukle lad," Mother said. "Don't worry, it'll be back you just see. It's probably found it's self a girl friend."

Many years later, after I had married, I found that my mother had paid Uncle Jack Varey to take the dog in his car and drop him off in Congleton, many miles away. I never saw Nigger again. I would never do that to a child of mine, or a dog for that matter.

*   *   *   *   *

Travelling during the summer were the best times. Sam Lock, Jim Varey and Jim Monks were our regular travelling companions. Our usual run would take in parts of Staffordshire, Lancashire, Cheshire, South Yorkshire, Derbyshire and Nottinghamshire.

The first horse I can remember was an aged mare called Dolly. Half legged with a bit of blood, she stood about thirteen two hands. Not quite big enough for a waggon horse, she was nevertheless a good and willing worker. With the waggon stuck in soft ground, the only way she could move it was to rear up in the shafts and take a leap forward. This usually got the waggon moving all right but was very hard on the harness.

Pulling off a muddy stopping place one day, a Gypsy man called Harry Watton insisted in yoking a little thirteen hands mare, heavy in foal, to our waggon. "It'll save you breaking your bits of straps," he said. Probably he just wanted an excuse to show off his mare. Certainly she was worth showing off. Black and white, well marked with plenty of feather to her legs, she pulled our waggon out of the mud an inch at a time. Sadly, I heard she subsequently lost the foal.

When Dolly saw a hill in the road ahead she would set off with the waggon at a fast trot. The momentum would get her so far up before she had to scratch and scrape to reach the summit and have a blow. I remember her slipping and going down in the shafts on one particular nasty hill. She suffered no serious injury; but chipped her knees. Dad rubbed soot into the cuts to make the wounds less visible, lest the cruelty man should stop us for ill-treating the mare.

No two days were the same when we were travelling, so it's difficult to write of a typical day. Aged ten or eleven, for me a day in summer might go like this. Up around seven thirty, Mother and Father having risen earlier. Dress and down the waggon steps. Dad is having a wash and shave in a small bowl on the waggon frontboard. Mother is cooking bacon on the outside fire and the kettle is on the kettleprop, singing merrily. If I'm lucky and we have some of yesterdays milk left that hasn't gone sour, I settle down to breakfast. Should there be no milk my first job is to go to the nearest farm and fill the little enamel can we have for the purpose. At other times we'd have Nestle's sweetened condensed milk in our tea, but we preferred fresh milk when we could get it.

I liked fetching milk. Most farms still used horses and I liked to see them going about their work. Other animals on the farms were also of interest to me and I would chat to the farmers about them. Cow sheds, or shippings as we called them were always warm in winter and cool in summer, and whilst I waited, the farmer would run some milk through the cooler, fill my can and take my sixpence.

Cows were mostly milked by hand, electric' milking machines being something of a rarity. Sometimes I would have to wait for the farmer to finish milking a cow before he could serve me.

"Won't be a couple of minutes son," he would say, with his head pushed into the hollow of a cow's flank and I would sit on a spare stool chatting to the farmer and listen to the steady swish, swish, as the milk went into the bucket.

"I saw cows being milked with a machine the other day," I volunteered to one farmer, as I waited for my milk. "It was doin' two at a time."

"Machines aye?" retorted the farmer. "I wouldn't 'ave one on the place if they gid it to me. Taint natural. Not many cows'll tek to them contraptions, you wait an' see. It just ain't natural. Anyhow, them'll not catch on; not round these parts them won't."

Coming out of a shipping one morning with my milk can in my hand, I tried to take a short cut across a corner of the yard that looked like hard packed earth. The earth turned out to be cow dung, four feet deep with a three-inch crust on top. I sank to my chest.

The laughing farmer pulled me out, stripped me and hosed me down with the powerful hose he used to clean the shipping. His wife gave me an old pair of trousers and a jumper, both several sizes too large. My milk can was irretrievably lost in the muck.

Carrying my boots between finger and thumb, I walked home barefoot. Being the only footwear I possessed, the boots had to be washed, dried and pressed into service again. Everyone seemed to think this incident hilarious, I saw nothing funny about it.

There's nothing like the taste of fresh milk, straight from the cow. I would often sneak a sly drink from the can on my way home. Not too much mind, or I'd be in trouble with Mother.

After breakfast, and a wash if I couldn't avoid it, I'd be off to see to the horses, moving them down a tether's length to enable them to get at fresh grass. The dogs would be allowed to accompany me on this trip and the job often turned into a rabbit hunt.

One of the terriers would bolt a rabbit from a hedgerow or bush and the lurchers would be after it in a flash. Should there be too much cover the rabbit would get away, but with a fair run, a dog would soon have it and bring it back to me. Rabbits were always welcomed by someone back at the camp. They're not to my taste however so I always gave mine away.

Horses attended to, it would be time for the business of the day. If Mother was hawking wooden flowers she would dye them in a two bowls of hot water in which she'd dissolved a couple of Drummer dyes, one of daffodil yellow and one of pillar box red. Should she be selling clothes pegs she would clip them on lengths of willow bark, a dozen to a strip.

When a pony and cart was available, all the women that were going out that day would pile onto it and drive to their hawking. Otherwise they would walk to the nearest village, or if going further afield, to the nearest 'bus stop.

Having reached their destination they would then hawk their wares, perhaps begging a few cast off clothes or some items of food along the way. Tea, sugar and butter were always welcome. Occasionally one of the women would come across someone who wanted their fortunes telling.

Money from this was usually shared amongst the group. Hawking done for the day, they would get the day's shopping and make their way home.

Dad would be off on his grinding 'bike for a day sharpening. His 'bike would have a grindstone clamped to the frame in a bracket. Wired into the back wheel would be a rim made from a large pram wheel with the spokes removed. This rim took a belt to drive the stone. Jinney Band, a kind of cord, usually procurable from ironmongers' shops, was used for the belt. Should Jinney Band not be available, builder's line would do. To complete the contraption, a stand was fitted to raise the back wheel from the ground and keep the 'bike upright when in grinding mode. Grinding finished, it was only necessary to slip the belt off, push the 'bike off its stand and it was ready to ride as an ordinary 'bike, the stand now forming a carrier.

Dad was very good at his job and had regular customers in many areas. He would sharpen not only knives and scissors, but garden shears and lawnmowers too. I accompanied him often and learned a trade that has stood me in good stead on many occasions.

Days when I wasn't going grinding with Dad were the ones I liked best. There was always plenty to do at home, but I enjoyed doing it.

Horses had to be watered. Often this involved taking them to a nearby stream or perhaps a pond, and on occasion, a farmer's water trough. There was always one horse that the rest would follow, so I would ride that one and let the others run loose, dragging their tethers. Traffic wasn't a problem; very few cars used the country lanes in which we stopped. Frequently a day would pass without site of a single car.

Cutting elder to make wooden flowers or willow for pegs was another daily chore, but one that I didn't mind. Hunting along a stream bank for willow, or a hedgerow for elder could be combined with a bit of rabbiting. Water for drinking I would bring in specially made cans, or jacks as we called them. Goodwin, a tinsmith in Sutton-in-Ashfield made our two. They held about five gallons each and were quite heavy when full. I would slip their handles onto the handlebars of my 'bike and wobble off to the nearest farm.

Keeping the fire going and laying in a stock of firewood would keep me busy for the rest of the day, or at least 'till my parents got home. When a few of the other children were at home, the work was more fun. We all had similar jobs to do and would unite to get them done and leave more time for play.

The kettle would be simmering on the kettleprop when Mam and Dad got home. Mother would wash her hands and immediately start to prepare the main meal of the day - frequently some kind of meat. Chops or sausage perhaps when available. Perhaps she'd part prepared a stew in the morning and it only needed the addition of potatoes and such to complete it. Whatever the meal, it would be supplemented with thick slices of bread and we would sit on the grass round the fire to eat it. Everything was cooked and eaten outside except in the severest of weather.

Much of our food was gathered from the fields. Never thinking of it as stealing, we would gather in season: Mushrooms, turnips, cabbage, swedes, carrots and potatoes, in fact all the commonly grown vegetables. Only enough for a meal or two were taken at any one time, we didn't have the facilities to store much. Bird eggs were also collected: Pheasant, water hen, duck and partridge. Partridge eggs are particularly nice and were my favourite. With the odd rabbit or hare, and now and then a hedgehog, we rarely went short, even during rationing.

After the evening meal, the men and boys would set to making pegs or wooden flowers to be ready for next day. If it was to be pegs I would have already peeled off the bark from the willow rods earlier in the day and stood them up teepee fashion to dry in the sun. Willow bark is best peeled with the teeth and comes off in long strips. Now I would chop the rods off into two peg lengths and pass them to father for tinning. When the pegs were tinned, I would chop them into single pegs and pass them back to Dad to be split and mouthed.

Should flowers be the order of the day my job was to saw the elder into the right lengths to make two flowers. Dad would then make the most beautiful chrysanthemum type flowers. Holding the flower knife against his right knee and the elder in his left hand he would quickly strip the bark. Holding the knife still against his knee and turning the elder as he shaved he would then carry on to make the flower head. Two-dozen flowers or two-gross of pegs were usually required.

Many of the families stopping with us would be similarly engaged but one by one, as they finished their jobs, many of the men would gather round one of the fires to talk.

'Ave yer bin out?' one man would ask of another.

'I had a couple of hours,' might come the reply.

'Do any good?' the first man would continue.

'I got a bit of bread,' was the inevitable answer. No matter how successful or otherwise a man's day may have been, the reply to any query as to what he had earned, was always, 'I got a bit of bread.'

The day's events would be discussed and stories told of bygone days and deeds. Sometimes a bit of dealing would take place. Horses, carts, chickens, cagebirds, dogs, waggons, carts and harness were all likely to be bought and sold round the fire, with many shouts of encouragement from the others present.

Anyone listening from a distance could be forgiven for thinking a violent argument was taking place. Gypsy men talk very loudly, with much waving of the arms. Mostly it was good-natured banter and every so often the circle of men would erupt in a roar of laughter. Should the deal not be concluded there and then, it would probably be adjourned to the pub. This kind of behaviour often got Gypsies barred from public houses, the landlord, judging by the raised voices that trouble was brewing. Not a bit of it, it was just normal conversation to them.

Children would play their endless games or sit around the fire listening to the men talk. In this way they would learn about their history and ancestors along with a valuable lesson in the value of horses and other trade goods.

All children were taught to respect their elders, older men and women being addressed as 'Aunt' and 'Uncle', even though they be of no relation.

Gypsy children were often threatened with extreme violence by their parents. They took not the slightest notice, knowing it to be all bluff. For instance, should a man be seated round a fire, and a small child walk between him and the fire, (very bad manners) the child's father or mother might say, 'There's a higerant child, come out of the man's face will yer? When I gets 'old on you I'll rip yer neck out.' The child might then laugh and run away in mock fear, but knew that to be the end of the matter.

Small children would be strip washed by their mothers beside the outside fire, before being packed off to bed in the waggon. We old men of seven or eight were allowed to wash ourselves and stay up 'till dark.

*   *   *   *   *

Travelling in winter was an entirely different matter. Life on the roads then was very hard. Grinding was a very poor trade now that almost no garden tools were in need of sharpening. We had to make do with mostly knives and scissors, and at ninepence and a shilling each, (four and five new pence respectively) earnings were very low. Picking potatoes and other odd farm jobs helped out, when we could get them. In the run up to Christmas, Mother would be selling crepe paper flowers. All the family, sitting in the waggon cosy and warm, listening to the wireless, would make these.

Batteries for the wireless were expensive - by our standards anyway. Ours needed a huge one hundred and twenty volt battery weighing about ten pounds, a smaller grid bias battery and a rechargeable wet cell called an accumulator. Most garages and radio shops had facilities to charge accumulators. Charging took around twenty-four hours and cost about a shilling.

Feeding horses was a constant problem in winter, corn was rationed and we couldn't afford to buy it anyway. Many times we've slipped the horses into some farmers field after dark, 'puvin the gries' we called it - a puv is a field and a grie a horse. This necessitated getting up before first light to remove them. Haystacks in isolated fields were visited under cover of darkness and a large sack filled.

Sam Lock and I were walking along a hedge side in the dark when we heard running footsteps behind us and the sound of someone coughing. We were both carrying large bags of hay removed from a stack a couple of fields away. With one accord we dropped the sacks and ran, wading through a small but icy stream on the way. Stopping to listen on the edge of a small coppice, we could detect no sound of pursuit. Creeping back after recovering our breath, we found a bunch of cows contentedly chewing our stolen hay. Cows cough just like a man we learned.

Coal was collected for the waggon stove, I don't remember ever buying any. Walking along a railway line it was possible to pick a bag of coal in half an hour or so. It fell from the steam-powered trains. If the driver of a slow moving train saw you standing by the track with your bag in your hand, he knew what you was doing and would often throw a few large lumps off for you.

Roadsides where steamrollers had been working were often a source of coal or cinders. Roller drivers often couldn't be bothered to pick up all the bits of fuel when they finished work so we would clean up after them.

Gypsies, and others of 'no fixed abode' were issued with emergency ration documents. 'Mergencys' we called them. For many items the shopkeeper would cancel them with a rubber stamp once the goods had been supplied. Mother would sometimes erase the stamp with bleach and present them in a different shop.

Another way of obtaining extra food was to meet soldiers coming home on leave at the local railway station. Soldiers always seemed to have plenty of emergency coupons and would sell some for a few shillings.

Uncle Billy came back to England once the war was over, having served his time for bigamy. Having no identity card and no ration allocation, he perforce stayed with us for a time. My parents provided him with food and shelter so they needed any extra rations they could obtain.

Coming back drunk one night he blacked Dad's eye in a scuffle. Next morning Mother told him to find alternative accommodation. He left a few days later and we didn't see him again 'till we were wintering at Hancock's. All must have been forgiven however, for Dad built Billy a waggon there. Dad was very good with a bit of wood and built quite a few waggons in his time.

*   *   *   *   *

Travelling wasn't always as straightforward as I may have made it seem however. The first question anyone asked on returning to camp was, 'Has anybody been?' Meaning, 'Have the police been to move us?' All too often they had. Sometimes we were ordered to move immediately, or, if we were lucky, we had until next morning to shift.

Many times we've had to move without the chance of a cup of tea or a meal after a long day's work. Then after yoking up and moving on, to pull out, as making camp was called, late at night, all the usual jobs had to be done.
Horses had to be tethered, and watered when they had cooled down - watering a sweating horse could bring on colic. Drinking water had to be brought, water being too heavy to carry with us. With wood gathered and the fire made we would snatch a hurried meal and set to making flowers or pegs to be ready for next day.
Sometimes we would be forced to move two or even three times a day. It was no use pleading that you were tired or hungry, that cut no ice with the local bobby. He had orders to move you on and move you on, he would. The only thing that sometimes worked was pointing out that the horses were absolutely beat, as often they were. Horses mattered more than people it seemed - more than Gypsies anyway.

This brings to mind a day we were travelling in the Black Country. Our group of four or five waggons had been travelling all day, two attempts to pull out having been

16

thwarted by the police. Dusk was falling and the horses were so tired that when we stopped at a village off-licence for groceries, one of the horses lay down in the shafts, breaking them. Tempers were frayed and when a gaujo man approached and asked where we were going, one of the men rounded on him, saying, "What the 'ell as it got ter do wi' you?"

"Well nothing really," the man replied, backing away a little. "It's just that I own a field about a mile along this road. The grass is overgrown and I thought your horses could eat it off a bit. You could camp there if you wanted." Showering the man with profuse apologies, we accepted gratefully.

Grass grew about three feet high in the field and the horses revelled in being off the tethers. Water was on tap in the adjoining field where our benefactor was having a house built. Potatoes grew amongst the grass, a crop obviously planted and not harvested. This idyllic stopping place had one snag; we couldn't earn a living in the area. After a week of trying we reluctantly had to move on - at least the horses were well rested.

Spring 1947 found Sam Lock and Jim Varey travelling with their families along the Uttoxeter to Derby road. Jim's waggon was behind Sam's and a cart driven by Sam's son Peter brought up the rear. As the procession approached Tutbury, the bridle came off the horse pulling Jim's waggon. Now un-blinkered and seeing the load it was pulling for the first time, the terrified horse bolted. Jim jumped off the front-board in an effort to reach the horses head, but catching his foot in the trailing reins, fell under the waggon wheels. Francis, Jim's wife who was travelling in the waggon jumped down to assist him but also fell and the iron shod waggon wheels passed over her legs.

Sam Lock, travelling in the lead, knew nothing of this until the driverless waggon overtook him with the horse going at full gallop. Charlie, aged about nine was hanging out of the back window and shouting as he passed.

"Shall I jump? Uncle Sam, Shall I jump?"

"No! Stay where you are." Sam roared as the waggon careered on its way. Handing the reins of his horse to his wife Lina, he jumped down and set off in pursuit of the runaway.

Jim's horse was a young sixteen hands gelding and was going like a train, despite the heavy waggon. Slowly, Sam overhauled it and on reaching the horses head, clamped a hand over its nostrils forcing it to a standstill.

Jim and Francis were taken to Derby Royal Infirmary. Jim had a broken pelvis amongst other lesser injuries. Eventually, he was transferred to a military hospital to recuperate, courtesy of his war record. I'm not sure what Uncle Jim did during the war, but I do know he was at Dunkirk.

Aunt Francis spent about three weeks in hospital before being discharged into her family's care. Her legs were not broken but had deep grooves gouged out by the iron shod waggon wheels. Mother brought her and her waggon to stay with us at Hancock's, the better to attend to her wounds. These wounds healed very slowly and Francis was diagnosed as having sugar diabetes, brought on by shock it was said.

Jim was away for about three months convalescing. Apparently the damage to his pelvis had been difficult to repair - leaving him with a pronounced limp.

Aunt Francis was visited by the doctor at Hancock's yard, sometime in 1949. She had been vomiting and I heard Mother say the vomit looked like excreta. The following morning, Francis' daughter Lizzie found her dead in bed. Mother told me the cause of death was given as peritonitis, something to do with a burst appendix.

Charlie and I were given 'bus fare and told to find as many relatives as we could. We found Aunt Lina and Uncle Sam stopping near the Michelin works in Stoke-on-Trent. Johnny Finney, old Vitus's brother, along with some of his children we found stopping at the Boundary, near Cheadle, Staffs. Old Johnny stopped a lorry and got us a lift into Newcastle-under-Lyme and from there we made our way home - it had been a long day.

Francis was buried in the little cemetery in Chesterton. Thereafter Jim travelled mostly with us, bringing up his little family on his own.

When stopping at Hancock's I had to go to school and around this time I was attending 'Broadmeadows Secondary Modern School for Boys' to give it its full title. I had passed an exam' that enabled me to go to a grammar school in Newcastle but my parents vetoed the idea. Preferring to go to school with my friends, I didn't mind this at all.

Monday dinner times were best at Broadmeadows. We had an hour and half for dinner and several of us would catch the 'bus into nearby Newcastle for the livestock auction. Grandad Vitus would be there without fail - drunk as a lord and best avoided. We helped farmers load cattle into trucks, rode horses up and down for the dealers and watched the strong man bend iron bars by beating them across his forearm, before handing them around his audience and inviting them to try and straighten them. It was with some reluctance that we would drag ourselves away in time for the 'bus back to school.

Homework was rarely given out at Broadmeadows, but on one occasion the class was asked to write a poem on any subject and bring it into school the next day. I wrote the following:

Soverein Lady.

The wind it whistled through the trees,
And whipped to foam the once calm seas.
The breakers thundered on the reef,
Where Soverein Lady came to grief.
She struck with a resounding crash,
And boiling seas poured through the gash.
The crew all ran to lower the boat,
But in that sea, it couldn't float.
And long before the night had fled,
The Soverein Lady's crew were dead.

Along with the rest of the class I handed in my poem the next day and thought no more about it. When the class was dismissed however I was asked to stay behind. Wondering what I'd done wrong I waited apprehensively for the class to leave. As the last pupil left the teacher beckoned me over.

18

"From where did you get this poem?" he asked.

"I wrote it last night like you said," I told him.

"Oh, I don't think so. I don't think so," the teacher stared at me intently. "You got it from a book, didn't you?"

"No sir," I protested. "I wrote it myself."

"And where did the name Sovereign Lady come from?"

"From the pictures sir. This cowboy 'ad a stallion called Golden Sovereign and a friend of mine's got a mare called Lady. I thought if they 'ad a foal together, a good name for it would be Sovereign Lady. I remembered the name when I was writing about the ship sir."

"Hmm," said the teacher. Apparently unconvinced. "Go on then, run along home. Oh! By the way, you've spelled sovereign wrong. Find out how to spell it and show me tomorrow."

"Yes sir," I called out, halfway through the door.

I had thought that to be the end of the matter but a couple of days later a teacher in another class called me out.

"That poem you say you wrote," he began.

"Yes sir?" I queried.

"I was reading a book of poetry last night and came across that poem. You didn't write it at all, did you? I think you're telling us lies. Aren't you?"

"I'm not a liar sir," I retorted. Then, as the thought struck me, added, "But you are."

"Go and sit down McCready," the teacher said. "Let's hear no more about it."

Back in my seat I was glad the episode was over and wished I hadn't shown the poem to the teachers.

'Broadmeadows Secondary Modern School for Girls' was adjacent to the boy's school and a high wooden fence separated the playgrounds. Playing football in the playground with a tennis ball, I inadvertently kicked the ball into the girl's section. The unwritten rule was that the boy kicking the ball over the fence must retrieve it. Climbing the fence, I saw a girl pick the ball up and run off with it. When I chased her she threw the ball to another girl and she to another and I was piggy in the middle. When I finally caught a girl in possession of the ball, she stuffed it up her knickers leg. Encouraged by the boys lining the fence to recover the ball, I did.

Someone reported me and I was sent to the headmaster's study and caned. Worse, I was then made to go to the girl's headmistress and apologise. Then I had to sit in with a class of girls doing needlework for the rest of the day.

The cane was used freely at this school and in general was accepted by the pupils. Names of boys so chastised were supposed to be entered in the punishment book, but in practise, only those caned by the headmaster were so recorded.

Calling me out, one Friday, the art teacher bent me over and caned me hard without explanation.

"What was that for sir?" I asked.

"You know, now get back to your seat," was the reply. But I didn't know, and still don't. Hurt more by the injustice of it than by the actual caning, I walked out of the class and out of the school, with the teacher running after me calling, "McCready! Come back hear this instant. McCready!" I ignored him and carried on walking. He

19

sent two boys after me but I refused to return. I didn't tell my parents about the incident, I didn't want Mother going to school and making a fuss. She would, had she known.

Attending school the following Monday, I expected to be questioned about the event, but it was never mentioned again. Thinking about it now. I don't remember ever being caned again, but then, I left school for good soon after.

Shortly before I left I was picked to swim for the school in an inter-school swimming gala held at Newcastle-under-Lyme public swimming baths. Two lengths crawl was my event and as I stood on the starting line I looked round the balcony to see it packed with spectators. As soon as I dived in I felt my borrowed swimming trunks slip round my ankles. All I could do was kick them off and carry on.

Touching home third, I swam back and recovered my trunks, slipping them on under water. When I climbed out of the pool, the applause from the balcony was deafening and I scurried back to the dressing rooms holding my trunks up and covered in embarrassment.

Walking home from school a couple of days later, I met Cousin Annie Winters coming in the opposite direction.

"Your waggon's burnt down," she said, as soon as she saw me.

"Is anybody hurt?" I asked anxiously. "'Ow did it 'appen?"

"Your mam's burnt her arms a bit, but it's not bad. I don't know what started it. You'd better get off home as quick as you can."

Hurrying home, I found things not as bad as I'd feared. All the print, felt and canvas covering of the waggon had been destroyed. Paintwork was blistered and clothes had been burned but the waggon bows and main fittings were only scorched.

Mother, it turned out, had left a primus stove burning and had been chatting next door when the flames were spotted. A small crowd soon gathered, running with buckets and bowls filled with water from a nearby pond. Against everyone's advice, Mother went into the flames and threw the burning primus out. She then tore down the blazing print and felt, throwing out anything she could. Luckily, she suffered only minor burns to her arms, but most of our few personal possessions were destroyed.

Dad came home to find Mother crying, sitting in the blackened waggon. Fortunately we had a shed to sleep in and friends and relations to help out where they could. Next morning my parents went shopping for a few essentials, Mother wearing a coat with only one sleeve -the other having been burned out.

Within a couple of weeks the waggon had been restored, and with it's new canvas top, looked very smart. Everyone said we had been lucky to get off so lightly, but I don't think luck had anything to do with it; it was mother's courage that saved the day.

Shortly after Aunt Francis died, Dad bought a mare to pull the waggon. Dapple grey, she stood about fourteen two hands high. Quiet and sound, she was 'a good worker in all gears' as the saying went. Her only fault was that when anyone tried to put a bridle on her, she would hold her head as high as she possibly could. Dad being a small man, just couldn't reach her, so, being a bit taller, I would harness her. We called her Blue because of the blue dapples she had in her summer coat.

Jack Toogood had a place next to Hancock's. He also had as good a set of London harness as you could wish to see. Black with red piping, it had white metal horse shoe-buckles and a patent leather saddle. Dad wanted this harness for Blue, but Jack wanted too much for it and they couldn't deal.

The night before we were due to shift, Jack came round to see us.

"I 'ears you'm all shiftin' tomorrow is yer?" Jack opened.

"Yep, were of in the morning," Dad replied.

"What's you'm gonna do with that ol' shed?" Jack wanted to know.

The old shed was one Dad had made from scrap timber he'd scavenged from somewhere. It was well built and I used to sleep in it.

"It's for sale," Dad said. "Would you buy it Jack?"

"Depends 'ow much it is," Jack muttered, walking round the shed and examining it. "It's only a bit of waste wood. You couldn't ask a man a lot fer it."

"It's as solid as a rock and bone dry," Dad told him. "I wouldn't let my lad sleep in it if it wasn't. Anyhow, how much would I have to give you to chop (swap) for them old straps of yours?"

I don't know how they dealt, but deal they did. Dad was delighted for he'd been planning to abandon the shed when we moved.

Jack came round early next morning, with a pony and cart to collect his shed. Not being sectional, the shed had to be manhandled onto the cart in one piece. This was achieved with much cursing and grumbling by a gang of helpers recruited from the other waggons.

The nervous little twelve hands pony Jack had yoked in the cart, was fidgeting from one foot to the other and rolling it's eyes, obviously upset by all the noise and shouting as the shed was loaded. Precariously balanced, it was then slowly pulled to Jack's place, just the other side of the hedge, by the quivering pony.

Once there, the gang of men stood debating where to put it whilst the sweating pony stood trembling in the shafts. Dylus Toogood, a lass of about twelve or so, went to the pony's head to try and soothe the poor beast. As she reached for the pony's bit, Jack saw her.

Roaring "Dylus!" at the top of his voice, he ran towards her. The poor pony could stand no more. Jack running towards her and the sudden shout was the last straw. She bolted.

Before she had gone fifty yards, someone got to her head and stopped her. Too late to save the shed however. Falling off the cart with a crash, it started rolling down a grassy bank, bits flying off as it went, to finish up a total loss in Jack's rockery.

Jack chased a screaming Dylus round the garden, shouting, "You'm done it now, anner you Dylus? You'm satisfied now, anner you Dylus?"

The gang of helpers quietly walked away.

* * * * *

Around this time we undertook a journey that I remember vividly to this day. Chesterfield was the starting point and the destination, Cheadle in the Potteries. The sensible route, and one that we had travelled many times before, was via Derby and Uttoxeter. For some reason, on this occasion, it had been decided that we would go 'over the tops'.

Travelling in company with Sam Lock, Jim Varey, Jim Monks and Mam's brother Billy, we set off - Billy had a waggon of his own now. After a hard day, we camped about three miles before Buxton-with the horses absolutely beat. Resting them for a day, we then continued through Buxton and took the road for Leek. The worst was yet to come.

Two horses were needed to each waggon for the long pull out of Buxton. A horse would be unhitched from one waggon, to be hooked alongside the horse in another. Chaining up we called this and it proved very hard work for man and beast. As the horses pulled, 'belly to the ground' was the horseman's term for this supreme effort, everybody, men, women and children pushed. Frequent stops were made to let the horses blow. My job then was scotching up, placing a wooden scotch under the wheel as the waggon stopped to take the weight off the horses whilst they rested. Having gained the summit, people and horses returned to the bottom of the hill to repeat the performance with the next waggon.

Four days hard work eventually saw us at the Boundary, near Cheadle, a journey that we could have accomplished in two taking the Derby route. People and horses were totally exhausted. I can still hear Jim Monks shouting encouragement to his horse, "Goo on Bob! Get on Bob! Good lad Bob! Go on Bob!" over and over again. Why did we do it? I just don't know. And when I ask the people who were the adults at the time, the only answer I get is, 'because we're dinglos.'

A Mr. and Mrs. Millwood ran the Boundary Inn then and they allowed us to camp in their field, adjacent the pub. Uncle Billy was a very good fiddle player and used to entertain at the pub during the evening. He'd once competed in a talent competition at the variety theatre in Stockport and there a theatrical agent saw him and persuaded Billy to go to London with him. Billy was going to be famous, he said. Billy returned to Stockport a few days later, fitted out with new shoes, a suit and overcoat. "I couldn't stick that London," was his only explanation.

Billy was a huge success at the pub - people came from miles around to hear him play. Cars filled the car park and lined the lane-such was the attraction. Ever the Romeo, Billy made several conquests amongst the local ladies and before long it was time for him to be moving on. Despite the pleas of the landlady, Billy moved, the rest of us staying a few more weeks.

Trying to get my thoughts in order, odd snatches of memory come to me and I don't know just where they fit in. For instance, I remember pedalling my 'bike for miles around country village shops in search of cigarettes for my parents.

'Bring anything,' they would tell me. 'Except Pasha.' These apparently being particularly foul. Woodbine, Craven A, Capstan, Robin, Turf and Park Drive all being acceptable.

Another memory is of a violent storm one winter's night. We were stopping on some common or other, and the gale force wind was hitting the waggon side on, threatening to blow us over. Roused from bed in the middle of the night, I found the camp alive with Gypsies trying to turn their waggons so as to present their backs to the wind. Waggons are very unstable when the lock is turned ninety degrees and the front wheels come parallel to the waggon. Several people had to try to hold the waggon from blowing over whilst others quickly pulled it round, 'arse ter t'wind'. With everyone helping, all the waggons were turned without damage.

Then there was the time when Sam Lock was making a grinding 'bike. Sitting with the 'bike on it's stand, he was pedalling away and the stone was fairly humming. Suddenly the stone exploded and bits of it flew for yards. One piece went through the side of a wooden shed and made a neat bullet hole. Another hit an alsation dog in the head, inflicting injuries from which the poor animal subsequently died. Sam was lucky, the small piece that hit him struck the heavy brass buckle of the belt he was wearing. Badly bruised, he perforce spent a couple of days in bed, but no permanent damage was done.

Occasionally one of the youngsters would borrow his father's grinding 'bike and we'd have a day hawking in an effort to earn ourselves a bit of pocket money. Peter Lock and I were on our way home from a day's hawking round the Salt Box, near Sudbury. Riding along the A50 with me pedalling and Peter riding on the stand, we were stopped by a policeman in a car.

"And where do you pair think you're going? he asked.

"Hilton," I told him. "We're stopping in Hilton Lane. By the gravel pits."

"Yes, I know where you live," the policeman said. "But your not both riding on that 'bike you're wobbling all over the road. Now either one of you walks or you both walk, understand?"

"Yes, OK," we agreed. "We'll both walk from here. It's not far now."

"See that you do," said the policeman, getting into his car and driving off.

When the car had disappeared from sight, we again started to ride. After a few minutes the police car drew up behind us again. Without a word, the policeman got out of his car, removed the valves from our 'bike tyres and handed them to me before getting back in his car and driving off. We walked back to Hilton Lane, the policeman passing us once again with a toot on his horn and a merry wave.

Hilton lane was supposed to be haunted, at least it was according to Uncle Jack Varey.

Sitting round the fire that night, he told this story.

"It's 'ornted yer know, this lane," he began, lighting his cigarette with an ember from the fire.

"Never!" said one of the men sitting round the fire. "'Ow does yer mean?"

"Well, it were like this." Jack drew on his hand rolled cigarette until it was glowing to his satisfaction before continuing. "I was stopping in this lane two year ago, me an Jim Monks. You ask 'im the next time you sees 'im. We'd been to the pub 'an come 'ome 'an 'ad a bit of supper like, 'an I'd just got ter bed when all of a sudden somebody were shakin' the waggon shafts 'an shouting. 'Get up Jack! Get up man!' It were Jim. I jumps out of bed 'an slips me trousers on and went out ter see what was up with 'im. When I finds Jim 'e tells me the gries 'ad gone.

'No sign of 'em' 'e said. 'But the tethers are still down the lane.'

Well, we searched all over for 'em 'an ends up in that little wood just behind the gravel pits. I lost sight of Jim for a bit and calls out for 'im. Just then I sees 'im a bit in front 'an went after 'im, but 'e wouldn't wait 'an I 'ad a job ter keep up wi' 'im.

Then I comes ter this bob-wire fence, I never noticed Jim climb over it but I could see 'im a bit in front. 'Ang on a bit Jim, I shouts, 'an climbs over the fence ter foller 'im. I'd not took more than a dozen steps before I sinks up ter mi waist in a bog. If it 'adn't a been fer a little bush growin' near the edge, I'd never a got out. I got 'old of a bit of a branch an just managed ter pull miself clear. When I gets out I shouted at the top of mi voice fer Jim thinkin' e'd gone down in the bog." Jack paused for effect and looked round his attentive audience. "Jim answers from way back in the wood." Stopping once again to re-light his cigarette, he continued. "That's when I knew."

"Knew what?" asked one of the men, impatiently.

"I'd been follerin' the devil," said Jack. "Stands to reason. That's the only way 'e could walk through a bob-wire fence, an that's why 'e never went down in the bog. Anyhow, if it weren't the devil I was follerin', who was it?"

Receiving no reply, Jack went on. "I went all of a shiver an shouted for Jim again. When 'e comes I tells 'im what 'ad 'appened an' I think it must of atrashed (frightened) 'im as well 'cos 'e said we'd better leave the gries 'till mornin' an' we'd find 'em then. When we gets back to the waggons, there was the 'orses eatin' a bit of grass like nothin' 'ad 'appened. An' I'll tell yer sumat else," Jack got to his feet and pointed down the lane to where the horses were tethered. "Them tethers 'ad never been undone. The chains were still tied to the 'edge an' the neck-straps was still buckled. So 'ow did them gries get loose? Tell me that. 'Ow did they get loose? I tell yer mate, I wouldn't stop 'ere on me own not for a pension I wouldn't and that's a fact."

As soon as Jack's tale was finished, someone chipped in with a story of his own, and so it went on round the fire, each man trying to outdo his neighbour in tales of ghostly happenings.

* * * * *

Bird catching was a hobby of many of the older Gypsy men and the pungent smell of birdlime being made on an open fire often filled the air at the right time of year. I won't give the recipe fore birdlime as catching songbirds is now illegal. Perhaps it was then, I don't know, and it probably wouldn't have made any difference anyhow. Goldfinches were the favourite quarry, much prized for their song and gaudy plumage. Seven coloured linnets was one old name for them as was tailor birds, this because of their habit of sitting on a thistle and dipping their beaks in and out of the fluffy tops to extract the seeds, seeming for all the world to be sewing.

Brown linnets were also much sought after for their sweet song and both goldfinch and linnet cocks were crossed with hen canaries to breed mules that were superb songsters.

Care was taken to keep the young mules out of earshot of cock canaries so that they wouldn't pick up on the canary song, a good mule had to be all finch noted and any canary notes in it's song would detract from it.

Lime was not the only means employed to catch birds. Trap cages were favoured by many, with different types of cage being used to take different species. Usually a call bird was used to lure the victim and good call birds were highly prized.

Gypsies rarely used nets because of the time involved. Food had to be placed in a certain spot for several days to get the birds feeding there. Once a fair number of birds were visiting the site, a net was rigged early one morning that could be pulled over the feeding birds. Inevitably a few would escape, but this was all to the good.

"Never take 'em all at one pull?" one old man advised me. "Alus leave a few go to tempt others back. Then you can 'ave another pull later on."

During my early teens I was heavily into rabbiting. I don't like rabbit to eat but I certainly enjoyed catching them. As soon as work was finished for the day, I'd be off and I often didn't return until the early hours of the morning. Cousin Charlie and his dad Jim were both keen rabbiters and often accompanied me. Being chased by irate farmers was part of the fun and we always managed to evade capture - except once.

We were stopping at Bilsthorpe in Nottinghamshire. Charlie and I had taken two running dogs and a couple of terriers off for an afternoon's fun. Walking along the edge of a wood, we came to a field newly set with some crop or other. Strung along the fence was a gamekeeper's gibbet containing crows, stoats, jays, a kestrel and other so called vermin. Laid out in the field, a little way from the hedge were two domestic cats. They had been shot and arranged in a lifelike position, with little sticks to hold their heads up. Obviously to frighten the birds off the crop.

Walking along the headland, we could see a police motorbike travelling along the road two fields away. Not unduly alarmed we nevertheless ducked back into the wood and watched. The motorbike stopped on the road almost opposite us, and, as we crouched lower; a Landrover with several men in it stopped behind it.

Peering through the bracken we could see men and policemen talking. Arms were waived in our direction so we decided it was time to disappear. Working our way through the centre of the wood we eventually came to a field on the other side. Three men, walking line abreast, were crossing the field in our direction. Creeping back into the wood, we stopped to consider our options. Breaking twigs and voices from the side of the wood where the gibbet was made our minds up for us. We ran. Bursting through the undergrowth into a path cut through the wood as a firebreak, we suddenly found ourselves surrounded by several men and were captured.

Searching us, one of the men asked, "What have you done with the pheasants? Where are the eggs? What have you done with them?"

Luckily we hadn't caught anything that morning, we' only been after rabbits anyhow, we didn't take pheasant during the breeding season. Our explanation that we were only taking the dogs for a walk and had decided to take a short cut through the wood on our way home was greeted with derision.

One of the men was sent to search the way we'd come in the hope of finding game we'd abandoned in our flight. We were marched off to a shed behind the large house at the top of a long drive and locked in.

"You'll be up before the magistrate in the morning," said the man we assumed to be a gamekeeper, as he locked the door.

"If we are," said Charlie." I'll tell about them cats in the field,"

"What cats?" said the keeper. "I know nowt about cats. I don't know what you're talking about." But we could see from his face that he did.

The shed was built like a log cabin and was much too strong to break out of. We settled down to wait. Talking, we decided that nothing much could happen to us because we hadn't caught anything. Nevertheless we were still worried.

"They could always do us for trespass in search of coney," I told Charlie.

"They've no proof," Charlie replied.

"They could invent some," I said. "They could say they saw us chasing rabbits. I wouldn't put it past 'em."

"As soon as someone opens that door, we'll make a run for it," I said.

"OK," Charlie agreed. "You try to get past him on that side and I'll try on the this. If one of us gets out he goes home and tells our dads. If we both get out we split up and make our way home separately, we'll 'ave a better chance that way."

"Right," I said. "I wonder what happened to the dogs?"

There was no way of knowing, and nothing to do but wait. Two or three hours must have elapsed before we heard a noise at the door.

"Ready?" whispered Charlie.

"Ready," I replied.

"The governor has decided to let you go," a voice said, as the man fiddled with the lock. "Now don't you let me see you around here again or you won't be so lucky next time."

Flinging the door open, a man we hadn't seen before beckoned us out.

"What about the dogs?" I asked.

"You can forget them," said the man. "You'll not see them again"

"We're not going without them," Charlie said.

"Go on, get off with yer," the man said. "We haven't got your dogs, we couldn't catch them. Now be off and don't come back. Think yourselves lucky you've been let go."

I wasn't surprised to hear the dogs had managed to avoid being caught - they were very wary of strangers and sure enough, the dogs came running to meet us as we approached the waggons.

We didn't return to Hancock's that winter but pulled instead onto Teaton's Bank, Sybil Teaton's camp. Many of my relatives were there, including Mother's parents. I remember Grannie Lizzie sitting on the waggon steps on a Sunday morning, reading the 'News of the World' to the dozen or so Gypsies gathered to listen. This I found to be a regular Sunday occurrence. The title of the newspaper was taken quite literally and it was generally conceded that if it wasn't in the 'News of the World' it probably hadn't happened.

Letters were delivered each morning to the camp and the postman came and parked his van in the middle of the camp and people would go and give their name and ask if there was anything for them. Aunt Lizzie asked one of my young cousins to go for her. "Ask him if he's any letters for Elizabeth Finney," she told him.

"Lizzie who," said the little boy. He'd never heard Aunt Lizzie called anything other than Aunt Lizzie.

"Elizabeth, Elizabeth Finney," Aunt Lizzie said.

Waiting his turn in the queue the child asked the postman, "'Ave you any letters for Lizzie buff Finney?"

"No, I'm sorry son, I haven't," said the postman, shuffling through the stack of letters.

"Well," said the boy. "'Ave you any for Lina buff Finney or Annie buff Finney then?"

Uncle Tom, Mother's brother, was on Teaton's Bank at this time. Tom's first born, Vitus, had been brought up by Tom's parents, Grandad Vitus and Grannie Lizzie. Jimmy was the eldest of Tom's children living at home and Jimmy and I were great pals, fetching water, picking coal and running errands together. Jimmy returned to camp one day to find his friend Pip's dad drunk and in a foul mood.

"Where's the water Pip?" Pip's dad demanded. "There's no water you idle little bastard. Now get some fetched or I'll give you idling about all day."

Pip had already brought water that day and had no idea why the water jacks were empty, they usually only needed to be filled once a day. Knowing better than to argue with his dad in that mood, Pip obediently went for more water.

On his return, his dad said, "Where do you think you've been? Does it take you all day to fetch a drop of water?" and taking the jacks from Pip, he emptied the water out. "Now get some more brought," he snarled. "And don't let it take you so long this time or I'll make you go again."

Behaviour such as this wasn't typical of Pip's dad and he was normally well liked and respected by his family. Goodness knows what got into him.

Incidents of cruelty such as this are extremely rare amongst Gypsies, which is probably why this one sticks in my memory. Generally, Gypsy children are well cared for, joining the adults in their work at an early age and are looked upon as valuable members of the community. Given the choice, I wouldn't choose any other way of life, and I don't know a Gypsy child that would.

Uncle Tom liked a drink, and would drive to the pub on a flat cart drawn by a mule. Leaving the mule tied outside, Tom would be in the pub 'till time was called. When at last he staggered out, three sheets to the wind as the saying goes, he would untie the mule, roll onto the cart and promptly fall asleep. With no hand on the rein, the old mule would deliver Tom safely home, crossing a busy main road in the process.

Tom and family eventually settled into a council house in Chesterton, where they became known as 'them bloody Finneys'. An excellent accordion player, Tom would entertain in the local pubs and was well liked by the gaujos. Several of his sons are musical and play guitar and sing. In fact, in later life, my wife and I liked nothing better on a Sunday than to drive over to Chesterton for a session in the pub with them.

One summer - I'd be about fourteen at the time - we travelled with Jim Monks, grinding in the little villages around Derbyshire and Nottinghamshire. Mother and her sister Lizzie were hawking lace and small-ware and I found it a very pleasant time. Towards the back end of that year, we camped in a little orchard behind 69 Town Street, Sandiacre, courtesy of the owner, a Mr. Stevenson. Turning the horses loose in the orchard, it was a pleasure to see them frisk and gambol in their delight at being off the tethers.

Jim and Lizzie, having no children at the time - they were to have a daughter late in life - I was the only Gypsy child there. Fortunately, I got on well with some of the gaujos, Mr, Stevenson's two daughters and a young man called Tony in particular.

Tony's parents were into amateur dramatics, and a bit upper crust. I don't think they approved of me. I introduced Tony to the delights of poaching, but when he took a pheasant and a couple of rabbits home, his parents were horrified and forbade him see me again - an order he frequently ignored.

Just a hundred yards or so from the orchard a wheelwright had a little business on the bank of the Erewash Canal and I spent many happy hours helping with various jobs. Jim Monks had two of the wheels from his openlot (Gypsy waggon with a canvas front instead of a door) left there for repair. They needed several felloes (sections of the wooden rim of the wheel pronounced 'fellies') replaced, and new steel tyres fitted.

"You can give me and Len a hand when we come to do them tyres later on today," the wheelwright told me. "It's easy to get a tyre on quick when there's three on the job." Len, it turned out, was the wheelwright's part time helper, a retired chap who lived a few doors away.

Hot steel tyres are lifted by means of metal bars with 'n' shapes in one end of them. Three of them are placed equal distance around the tyre and it then lifts easily and evenly. Large, cast iron, circular beds, set in the ground, support the wheel itself. When the tyre is white hot, it is lifted evenly and dropped onto the wheel. With not a moment to lose, the wheelwright then taps the tyre into place with a sledgehammer whilst his assistant follows him with buckets of water to quench the steel and stop the felloes bursting into flame. As the tyre cools it contracts and effectively holds the wheel together.

Pumping the bellows for a farrier who had a forge at one end of Town Street was another job that earned me a few shillings in my spare time.

Spring saw us on the move again and our first stop was Bulwell Common, now sadly a housing development. From there we moved to Larch Farm, near Mansfield, where we met up with Sam Lock, Jim Varey and Jack Varey. They were stopping in the lane we had intended to pull in. I was pleased to meet them for I would have the company of my cousins for a while, but Jim Monks wasn't. I don't know why, but then Jim was always a moody sort of man.

"I'm not stopping with that lot," he said, as soon as he saw the waggons. Consequently we pulled in a lane half a mile or so away. We'd just got pulled out; un-harnessed the horses and got a fire going when Sam Lock and company arrived with their waggons, pulling in the lane with us. Jim Monks was furious. Jumping up onto our waggon front-board, he shouted. "This is a made up affair and I'm not having it! You can stop with your breed if you want, I'm off." With that, he yoked his horse again and pulled away. No one knew what it was all about, but as I've said, Jim was a funny sort of chap.

Jack Varey had a dilapidated old car that he used for spivying (that is, painting farm barns with creosote and tar.) Sam Lock and Jim Varey were grinding but they told us they had been working with a Jim Crow, tatting. (Collecting rags woollens and scrap metal)

"There's good money to be earned," Sam told us. "It's better than grinding, as soon as I earn enough money for a pony and cart of my own, that's the job for me."

* * * * *

Shortly after, Sam and my father bought a pony between them, a sturdy little strawberry roan, twelve two with a flaxen mane and tail. Tommy Horse was an ex pit pony and one of the best workers I've ever seen. An old trap was acquired and for a few months, the two families worked together. We would all go together in the trap, to some village or town. Once there the women would hawk as usual and the men and boys would deliver hand-bills to the houses offering to buy any old rags or scrap metal. As soon as the bills were delivered, we'd all go back to the start and collect them up again, along with anything the householder wished to dispose of. This was hard work as we were walking from around nine-o-clock in a morning until four or five at night.

Then it was time to pick the women up and back to the waggons to sort the load, bag the rags and clean the non-ferrous metal of iron and other contaminants. It made for a very long day and we'd all be absolutely beat by the end of it.

Once again we spent the winter at Sandiacre, this time with Sam Lock. Chambers of Worksop were buying our scrap etcetera and Harry Chambers would send a lorry to wherever we were staying to collect our load. Two or three of us would ride with it, to 'weigh in' as we called it.

Having been paid, we would gather in a little cafe near the 'bus station in Worksop for a bite to eat and to divide the cash. With bellies and pockets replenished, we would then make our way home by 'bus. It was the highlight of the week.

Jack Varey brought news that Grannie Lizzie had died, and I travelled in Jack's old car with my mother and Aunt Lina, to their camp. They were stopping in Bradwell Woods, between Talk Pits and Longport, in the Potteries.

Custom decrees that relatives of the dead do not sleep on the night before the funeral, a custom known as sitting up. Grannie's coffin was in a waggon set a little aside from the rest. Candles were left burning and every so often one of us would go in and check all was well. It was the middle of winter and bitterly cold, so much so that ice formed on the inside of the waggon containing the coffin.

It would be around seven in the morning and still pitch black outside when I was sent to check the candles.

'If they're burning low, blow them out,' I was told. The candles were burning low, in fact one of them had gone out and so I started to extinguish the others. Inky blackness descended on me as I pinched out the last candle, and I was suddenly afraid. Stumbling down the waggon steps I ran towards the other waggons, only to stop short when a dark, man-like figure loomed in front of me.

"Who's there?" I called, but received no reply. With the hair on the back of my neck tingling, I set of at a tangent, crashing through the wood blindly. Scratched by brambles, and out of breath, I stopped to listen for sounds of pursuit and hearing none, began to calm down. Slowly and cautiously, I made my way back to the camp and slipped into one of the waggons.

"Was the candles all right," Grandad Vitus asked. "You've bin a long time, where've you bin?"

"The candles were low and I put them out Grandad," I said. "Afterwards I went in the wood to do a job for myself."

"Good lad," said Grandad. "Now go an' tell your Uncle Jack to light some more candles." Came the dawn and I found the dark shape I'd seen was an old overcoat thrown over the radiator of Jack's car in an effort to keep the frost out.

29

Spring found us once again on the move. Dad had bought a little coloured gelding called 'Fire', and the partnership with Sam Lock had been dissolved. Sam had bought Dad's share in Tommy Horse and each family now worked independently.

Fire, though pretty to look at, was nappy. That is to say he would pack in his job whenever he decided he'd had enough. When he did, no amount of coaxing or beating would change his mind. With legs locked stiff, he just stood there, refusing to move come what may. Sometimes he'd do this as soon as he was yoked. At others he'd work every day for weeks without complaint.

Eventually, we found that one way to move him when he played up was to tie his alter to the cart in front. Bracing his legs, Fire would resist as usual, but as the horse in front pulled, the pressure on Fire's neck would become intolerable and he would be forced to scramble forward to relieve it. After a while, Fire stopped napping when following another cart, but could never be trusted alone.

We had heard of a stopping place at Dinnington near Sheffield and decided to try it though it was outside our usual run. Pulling on to Dinnington Common, I was praying that Fire wouldn't nap and show me up to the dozens of travellers stopping there. My prayers were answered and Fire pulled the laden cart through the soft mud like a good 'un.

Amongst the Gypsies stopping there was a man I shall call Derby John. John had a little liver chestnut mare that I fancied and when I saw him yolking it up one day I asked him if he was going near a shop.

"I'll come with you and get some paraffin if you are," I said. What I really wanted was a chance to see his little mare go.

"'Ar! I'm goin' for fags," John said. "Get your can an' I'll give you a ride."
Once on the cart he handed the reins to me, saying,

"That's what you really wanted boy, wasn't it? You wanted to see her go, now hold her son, she's a bit hard mouthed, she'll be away with us if you don't watch her."
Hard mouthed she certainly was, but an exhilarating drive and I wanted her. I don't remember the details of the deal but suffice to say that I ended up with the mare in exchange for Fire. I gave John a few pounds to boot I seem to remember and I was well pleased. Dolly, as she was called, had only one fault - she wouldn't back up. That I was prepared to live with.

Later that year we bought a hackney gelding with a fancy long-winded name, we called him Billy. Billy was a handsome pony and a pleasure to see go with that peculiar hackney gait.

"Ee picks 'em up well, ee goes that 'igh all round," Sam Lock said when first he saw the pony, and indicated with his hand about four feet from the ground.

Prices for scrap metal, rags and woollens started to fall and by late autumn we were barely making a living. We moved to Cheadle in the Potteries and to help out I took a job at a nearby brick works. That would be late in 1951 for I was fifteen at the time. My job was to stand at the huge, noisy press, taking the bricks from the chute as they came sliding out and stacking them on a specially designed wheelbarrow. Green, or unfired bricks are very heavy, these being made of compressed 'marl', a type of clay. As soon as one barrow was full it would be wheeled of to the kiln and I would start to load the next barrow, already in place. Bricks came off the press at the rate of about one every two seconds and both bricks and myself being green, a few hours of this was hard on the wrists and back.

Just after our midday break on my second day, the bricks started coming off the press with the ends chopped off. One of the barrow wheelers noticed this and shouted, "Ends off! Ends off," at the top of his voice. Everyone took up his cry around and immediately, the press stopped. What a welcome relief. Whilst the problem was being fixed, one of the men told me that this sometimes happened when one of the wet bricks failed to clear the mould in time for the next brick to come along and the knock on effect chopped the end off all ensuing bricks. Setting up the moulds again took about fifteen minutes and I thought it was great.

After a day or so, I found that by letting three or four bricks build up in the delivery chute, and then just as a mould was about to deposit another brick onto it, pushing them back with my knee I could create an ends off situation. I employed this method of gaining a rest once or twice a day, thinking I was doing everyone a favour, until, during one stoppage I got talking to Pop, one of the barrow wheelers.

"That bloody machine wants sorting," he grumbled. "I'm sick of these ends off, I think them moulds want changing."

"What does it matter," I replied. "At least we get a rest, and I'm certainly ready for one."

"Never mind the bloody rest," snorted Pop. What about our bloody bonus? We must be two or three pounds down this week already."

I decided not to mention my little ruse with the press and the machine miraculously cured itself of the problem.

Winter seemed to drag on that year and I for one was glad when we were on the road again. Early spring found us in the Black Country, along with Sam Lock and Jim Varey.

During a long spell of wet weather, through which I had picked coal, moved horses and generally been soaked through several days on the run, I developed a pain in my left side.

We moved to Milford Common, on the edge of Cannock Chase and still in pain, I decided to find a doctor. I was told of a doctor's surgery in the grounds of a large park and after a long walk, I found it. The doctor refused to see me at first, saying I was not on his panel, but when I produced a medical card, I was told to wait until all the other patients had been seen and then I was called into the consulting room.

"You've got pleurisy," the doctor told me on completing his examination. "There's not much I can give you for it, you just need to go home and rest."
He then stuck a huge plaster across my lower rib cage and I found that this did ease the pain somewhat.

When I got back to the waggons, I found the police had been and we had to move. Over the next few days, we made our way to the Potteries and pulled onto a place called the Timber Yard in Chesterton. I felt much better with the plaster on my ribs, it stopped them moving and the pain wasn't too bad.

Cousin Vitus called one day and he and I decided to have a few days grinding together. Peddling my bike around Froghall the next day, I became so short of breath that it was as much as I could do to make the journey home.

31

"I'm off to the drabengro (doctor) again as soon as I get home," I told Vitus.

The doctor with whom I was registered had a surgery just a few hundred yards from our camp in Chesterton and as soon as he opened I presented myself there. He seemed very concerned when he examined me and, pointing to the plaster, asked, "How long have you been wearing that thing?"

"It'll be about ten days or so now," I told him.

"Your lung has filled up with fluid I'm afraid," he said. "It can be very serious. I'm going to ring for an ambulance and get you into hospital right away. Where are you living now?"

When I explained that I lived in the waggons that could be seen from the surgery window, he told me to go home and get some things together.

"The ambulance should be with you in ten or fifteen minutes," he said. "You'll want some pyjamas and probably some carpet slippers, and a toothbrush and toothpaste. You'll need to let your parents know where your going so walk home slowly and don't exert yourself."

Thanking the doctor, I walked home wondering what I would do about the things I was supposed to take with me to hospital. I'd never owned pyjamas, slippers or a toothbrush, but when I told my mother, she said she would buy them and bring them to the hospital that evening.

I was to spend about twelve weeks in hospital and during that time, Mother and Aunt Lina visited me on six or seven occasions. More frequent visits were difficult because the waggons were being moved on so often.

I remember winning the ward sweep when Gordon Richards won the Derby on a horse called Pinza, and watching the coronation of Queen Elizabeth on the hospital television set.

When I was discharged from hospital I was told to return at intervals during the next three years for physiotherapy sessions and check up x-rays. This I did, travelling from various parts of the country by 'bus and train. During my final check up, I was surprised when the doctor told me I was in the clear and that I could now start work - I hadn't realized I should have stopped.

*   *   *   *   *

Two or three four months after this my parents swapped our waggon for a trailer. With a wheel at each corner and a waggon type lock, it was like a small showman's waggon. No one in my family could drive a car so we had a tow bar fitted to the back of a dray and hooked the trailer behind that. With Blue in the shafts, and Billy chaining up, we travelled many miles.

Although I didn't realize it at the time, this was the end of an era for us, a time of change and a passing of the old ways - a passing I often regret.

Many Gypsy families were changing to motors and trailers around this time and it was decided that a driving licence was needed. Taking a driving test was an option not even considered - contact with authority of any kind was avoided whenever possible. It was rumoured that in Northern Ireland, driving licences could be had for the asking, so Sam Lock and I decided to ask.

It was March and the last of the snow had just about melted. We were stopping on Skegby Sands, a piece of wasteland above Kings Mill Hospital, near Sutton-in-Ashfield and Sam sold his dray for twenty-eight pounds to finance the trip.

Catching a 'bus to Nottingham, we then took a train to Liverpool, and from there the boat to Belfast. Docking in Belfast early next morning, we went in search of breakfast.

On the quayside, we found McCready's cafe.

"Come on Sam," I joked. "Let's eat at my place."

Being more than a little nervous about the forthcoming brush with officialdom, we ate but little.

Enquiring as to where the Gypsies camped around these parts, we were told, 'Ah! You'll find 'em down the Donegal Road, just ask for Bog Meadows an they'll be there to be sure.'

Wandering round Belfast, waiting for the shops to open, we came across an early opening barber's shop and Sam went inside for a shave. From the barber we learned that the driving licence office was in Ormeau Avenue, and that we would need a photograph to go on the licence.

Emerging from the barber's, we found the shops beginning to open and soon found a post office and got the licence application forms. Sure enough, photographs were required so we went in search of a photographer.

'Passport and Driving Licence Photographs - Ready in Three Hours' the sign said, when we found the shop.

Leaving the shop with three hours to kill, we decided to go to the pictures. The film was in 3D and as we entered, we were given coloured spectacles to wear. Sam resolutely refused to wear his and sat through the film seeing everything double. When we came out, he said it was a load of rubbish and he couldn't understand what people were getting so excited about. I told him he should have worn the spectacles but he said there was nothing wrong with his eyes and he could see as well as anybody.

We collected the photo's, and made our way to Ormeau Avenue, our forms already filled in with the address: Caravan, Bog Meadows, Donegal Road, Belfast.

"You go first, "Sam said. "See 'ow you go on, then I'll get mine."

Approaching the counter with not a little apprehension, I handed over my form and photographs. Handing me my licence with the photo' attached the clerk smiled at me and said, "Now don't be catching the boat back right away, will you?" Mumbling something in reply, I took my precious licence and hurried over to where Sam was waiting.

"What did he say? What did he say?" Sam asked anxiously.

"He told me not to catch the boat back right away," I said. "But he wasn't nasty about it. He was smiling, like it was a joke."

"That's it, I knew there'd be trouble, I'm not going for mine. Come on let's get out of 'ere before we get lelled (arrested)." Sam took my arm and ushered me out as he spoke.

"But we've come so far," I protested. "Just hand the papers over the counter and he'll give you your licence with no trouble, you see if he doesn't."

"I'm not going and that's that," Sam was adamant. "I should like to get miself locked up in a foreign country for a poverty drivin' licence an' never get 'ome. I'm not doin' it," he said with finality. Nothing I could say would change his mind and we caught the boat back that night with just the one licence.

Back home, Sam and Dad bought a car, a Sunbeam Talbot. Why they bought a car, I'll never know. A van or lorry would have been much more useful. Perhaps they thought a car would be easier to drive. I taught myself to drive in the quiet country lanes around Mansfield. Jack Varey gave me two lessons of about ten minutes each, and then I was on my own. After a couple of days, I began to get the hang of it.

Norman Smith, a dealing man from Bilsthorpe came and bought us up. Blue, Billy, Dolly, our dray and two sets of harness were sold in the one deal. Norman took the dray and the harness with him on his lorry and I undertook to deliver the horses next day.

By morning I was beginning to regret the sale of the horses, something I hadn't considered in the excitement of getting a motor car, but a deal's a deal. With a heavy heart, I mounted Blue, and with Billy and Dolly on either side, I rode to Bilsthorpe. Turning the horses into Norman's field, I watched them frisk about with the pleasure of being off the tethers, then I walked to the 'bus stop for the 'bus back to Skegby. Later, I heard that Blue had been sold to an old Gypsy woman who, in order to control, had starved her. The RSPCA had taken the woman to court, where she had been fined and banned from keeping horses for a number of years. Blue, I heard, had been taken to a home for abused horses where she spent the rest of her days. I often wish I'd gone to see her at the rest home. One shout of 'Blue' and she'd have come galloping up in anticipation of her favourite treat, a piece of bread.

News that scrap collecting was picking up again, prompted Sam and Dad to swap the car for an old fifteen-hundredweight Bedford van to use for that job. We were once again in partnership with Sam Lock's family, having the one van and one driving licence between the two families.

On our first trip with the van, we discovered that it used almost as much oil as petrol. In addition, after a mile or so the van would fill with a choking smoke that made eyes run and breathing difficult, even with all the windows wound down.

"I bet there's something wrong with it," said Dad, when we stopped and climbed out for air.

"Do you think so?" asked Sam, alarmed. "Let's take it to a garage and ask someone."

Controlling his amusement at our ignorance with great difficulty, the mechanic informed us that the engine was completely clapped out and the rest of the van wasn't in much better shape. His advice to us was, scrap it. Scrapping the van was not an option; we couldn't afford another, so an alternative solution had to be found.

"Let's ask Jack," I suggested. Meaning Jack Varey. "He's had a motor for months. He must know all about them by now."

"Yer best bet is ter find a secon' 'and engine," Jack said. "I'll 'elp yus put it in if yus get one."

Eventually an engine was located at Lister's car salvage yard in Chesterfield. It was in a Vauxhall car but we were assured it was the same as the engine fitted to our van.

"If you come back tomorrow, you can hear it run, and I'll have it cut out for you," said Charlie Lister. Fifteen pounds was the asking price, but after a lot of haggling, we bought the engine for twelve, subject to it running satisfactorily. Not knowing if we'd had a good deal or not, we agreed to return next day.

Jack was persuaded to accompany us the next day and give his expert opinion on the engine. We were stopping at Bilsthorpe at the time and our chosen route took us through Pleasley. Just through Pleasley, a policeman flagged us down.

"I wonder what 'e wants," Jack muttered as we drew to a halt. "If 'e sees all this smoke we'll be lelled."

"Where are you heading?" The policeman enquired.

"To Chesterfield," we replied in chorus. "Why?"

"Good," he said, opening the van door. "You can give me a lift." And with that, he climbed into the passenger seat as Jack moved into the back of the van to make room for him. Not knowing if we had the right to refuse, we carried on.

We hadn't gone more than two miles before he could stick the smoke no longer.

"Stop! Stop!" he cried. "Let me out of here. You'll all be dead before you reach Chesterfield in that thing."

"We're just goin' fer a new engine now," Jack explained.

Coughing violently, and with tears rolling down his face, the policeman, hardly able to talk, got out and waved us away.

With Jack's expert assistance, the engine took four of us, three days to fit. Once we had the engine in, we found that the gearbox wouldn't go on. Eventually it was discovered that the clutch plate had been fitted the wrong way round. Correcting this little mistake took another day, but finally the job was done. Several nuts and bolts were left over, but when we swung the starting handle, the engine fired first time. We experienced no further trouble with it.

Three months or so later, Sam decided he wanted a motor of his own and bought an old Morris lorry. I purchased Sam's share of the Bedford van. He and I then made another trip to Belfast to obtain a driving licence for him.

Belfast driving licences were valid for one year. They could be renewed by post if a covering letter was sent explaining that the sender was on holiday in England and would be returning to Belfast. We didn't think it prudent to use this ruse too often though. On the fourth anniversary however, application had to be made in person and new photographs submitted. Consequently, Sam and I made several trips to Belfast over the next few years to renew his or my licence. Had Sam obtained his licence on that first occasion with me, they would have expired together, and could both have been renewed on the one trip each time.

Eventually, when testing was introduced to Northern Ireland, a licence obtained there could be exchanged for an English licence and many Gypsies took advantage of this. I however had taken the English test a few months before.

When Sam started to drive, after a few short lessons from me, he had great difficulty changing down the gears. Almost all vehicles at that time were fitted with a gearbox known as a crash box. That is to say, there was no syncro-mesh on any of the gears and changing down was quite tricky. First the clutch had to be depressed and the gear-stick moved into neutral. Then the clutch was released and the engine revved to a speed to match the lower gear. Next, the clutch was depressed again and the gear selected before releasing the clutch again.

Sam hadn't quite got the hang of this and his lorry could be identified by the sound of protesting gears, long before it was in sight. When we talked about it and I explained the procedure to him for the hundredth time, he insisted that he was doing everything right and that the lorry must be at fault.

Riding with him one day, I noticed that when he put the gear-stick into neutral and revved the engine, he didn't release the clutch. When I told him what he was doing wrong, Sam insisted I hadn't told him to do that at that point. However, his gear changing improved greatly from then on.

*   *   *   *   *

Christmas of that year found us stopping on Mansfield Brickyard, along with a dozen or so other Gypsy families.

Hope Price was stopping there and had just bought a new trailer. This trailer was fitted with the new two-inch ball hitch, instead of the then usual pin and eye coupling. This new hitch was viewed with suspicion by the Gypsies gathered round when Hope was coupling up to move one morning. 'That's never safe,' and, 'I wouldn't trust to that. There's nowt ter 'old it on,' seemed to be the consensus of opinion. Hope was not to be swayed.

"I've brung it 'ere with that an' I'll take it away with that," he decided. "The trailer man told me them'll all be like that in a bit." So saying, Hope move off, and his advisors drifted away, shaking their heads.

Harry Smith, the insurance man from Worksop called on the camp one afternoon. He was looking for a Jack Varey he said, not knowing that Jack was standing beside him at the fire Jack had been involved in a motoring accident, Harry told us, and had failed to send in a claim form. Unfortunately, no one knew of Jacks whereabouts and so Harry turned to the man beside him at the fire and, stuffing a ten-shilling note into Jack's pocket said, "If you see Mr Varey, tell him to call in the office will you? And keep that for your trouble."

"Why thank you," Jack smiled. "I'll see 'e gets the message."

Mansfield Brickyard was where I first met my wife to be, Julie Booth. Louie Lock, Sam's daughter brought her to the camp and introduced us. I'd seen Julie about a year before when we had been stopping on Skegby Sands with Charlie Gaskin. Julie, then aged twelve had often visited Charlie's daughters. I hadn't taken much notice of her then.

Christmas Eve is Julie's birthday so she must have been thirteen when I met her on the Brickyard. She was very slim, extremely beautiful with a pair of bewitching blue eyes. I wouldn't say it was love at first sight, but I found her very attractive. We started going out together and as I got to know her better, I liked her personality. She was very mature for her age, if truth be known, more so than I.

The Bedford van was swapped for a Ford V8 Ex-WD ten hundredweight van that broke half-shafts with monotonous regularity, and soon after that we moved to Stairfoot, near Barnsley.

Julie and I had made no commitment to each other at this time, though Julie had given me a photo of herself taken on her school sports day. The snap of her winning the high jump had been taken by a teacher.

36

Stairfoot was a big camp of many years standing. Amongst the residents when we moved on were Old Devon Price, John Ayres, Nip Hamer, Rap Smith and George Booth - Julie's uncle. I knocked about with a crowd around my own age. There was Sam Price, his sister Ethyl, Brian Batty, Enoch Hamer, his sister Edna, Cilla Mitchell and one or two others whose names escape me.

Sam Price had got all Gypsies barred from the local cinema. He'd set fire to the fur coat of a gaujo girl, sitting in the seat in front of him, and then tried to extinguish the flames with a carton of pop.

"I didn't fink it'd burn like that," he said when he told me of the incident.

'Buses to and from town also operated a ban on Gypsies. I don't know the reason for this, like the one for the cinema; it was in place before I arrived. Sam decided to challenge the 'bus ban one evening, boarding a 'bus and refusing to leave. The driver took him to Barnsley police station where he was detained for a few hours and released with a caution.

Our Ford van broke yet another half-shaft and we had great difficulty finding a second hand replacement This being about the fifth we'd had to change, I think we were using up the available supply. One was eventually located in a breaker's yard in Wombwell and when I went to collect it I saw a Fordson van that I thought would suit our purpose better than the V8. After a little haggling, I bargained for it and, not having sufficient funds to purchase it outright, left a deposit on it.

Half-shaft replaced, we moved to Royston Common along with John Ayres, Sam Lock and Jack Varey. We were very short of money at the time - the V8 having eaten away most of our savings.

"We'll have to get stuck in and earn some money," Mother said. "We need that other van. You'll 'ave to nurse our van along until we can pay for the Fordson."

Get stuck in we did, billing Sheffield for scrap and such and working long hours every day. Luckily, Sheffield was good to us; we had a good run and managed to earn the balance needed to pay for the Fordson.

John Ayres bought the V8 from us and loaned it back to us in order that I might drive to Wakefield to tax the Fordson. On the way back, the half-shaft broke yet again. We never did discover the reason they broke so frequently - we'd even changed the complete back axle at one stage - but break they did. Typically, when I got the van towed back to Royston, John jumped up and down on the bonnet in temper. He then threw a car jack through the windscreen and tried to burn the van. When the fire he'd lit under the van went out, without the van catching alight, John swore there never was such an unlucky vehicle.

"It won't even burn," he complained. When he'd calmed down, he sold the van to a farmer he knew who wanted the wheels and axles to make a farm trailer with. The V8 engine fitted one of the farmer's machines. In the end John made a fair profit on the van, it wasn't so unlucky for him.

The Fordson turned out to be as big a load of trouble as had the V8 and I was soon looking round for another vehicle. John took me to a dealing man in Rotherham who usually had a lorry or two for sale. We met him in a pub and I bought a 1939 Bedford lorry from him.

"There's a spare gearbox to go with it if you want it," he told me. "It's in the shed behind our house. You might as well have it; it's no good to me now the lorry's gone. Here, nip and fetch it Son," and he handed me the keys to his shed.

His house was about a quarter of a mile away and I found it easily from his directions. When I tried to lift the gearbox I was surprised by the weight. Too embarrassed to admit it was too heavy for me, I struggled to carry the box back to the pub. How I avoided a rupture I'll never know, but somehow, I got it there. With my last ounce of strength, I heaved the gearbox onto the back of the lorry parked outside the pub and staggered inside to take a deep drink of the pint I'd left.

"You've been a long time Son," the dealing man looked at me and smiled. "What's the matter then? Wouldn't the 'owd lorry start then?" It was then I realized I'd been expected to take the lorry I'd just bought.

"Oh, I never tried it, I replied casually. "It didn't seem worth it just for a gearbox so I carried it.

"What! all the way from our house?" The dealing man shook his head ruefully. "You'll do yourself a mischief Son," he said. "That's how you end up with big balls."

"Gerraway!" I said. "It wasn't that heavy." But I was glad of a lift with it when I got it home.

Wakefield was our next stopping place. We moved to the common there with John Ayres leaving Sam and Jack Varey at Royston. Jimmy Berry was stopping at Wakefield and he happened to mention that Tommy Gaskin had a nice little Bedford lorry for sale. The lorry I had just bought was burning oil. Extensions had been fitted to the spark plugs in an effort to prevent them oiling up. Even so, they oiled every ten miles or so and would start misfiring. Then it was necessary to stop and clean the plugs, before motoring for another ten miles and repeating the performance. Consequently I swapped for Tommy Gaskin's lorry, paying him the difference. Apart from a couple of valves blowing, the lorry I got from Tommy turned out to be a good buy, and without doubt, the first good motor I'd ever had. John also had a Bedford lorry with valves blowing at the time. He and I took the heads off them both and ground the valves in.

As I was rubbing down the lorry prior to painting, Jimmy Berry sat watching me. "You know how that lorry would look well?" He asked.

"No uncle," I said. "How?"

"Paint the cab and body royal maroon and the mudgards signal red," he advised. I did as he suggested, and with new chrome strips on the radiator grill, the lorry did look well - a real eye catcher in fact. I could have sold it half a dozen times to the different men who asked me to put it on price, but having got a decent lorry at last, I was loath to part with it.

I was running short of handbills and I mentioned this to John. "Well I could do with some bills," he said. "I know a good printer's in Manchester. He's always got bills ready printed for the travellers. "We could catch a 'bus there from Wakefield 'bus station if you like."

Next morning we caught the early morning 'bus and arrived in Manchester about nine thirty.

"I'm sorry, I've only got two thousand ready," the printer told us. "I'll have more tomorrow if that's any good."

Of course, tomorrow wouldn't do, so we took what he had ready. John's thousand pack had everything we collected mentioned whilst the pack I finished up with omitted scrap iron.

"These are no good John," I complained. "There's no scrap on them."

"You can always ask for a bit of scrap," John said. But he made sure he had the good bills. Not that I blame him, had the situation been reversed I'd probably have done the same. Travelling home on the 'bus, John dozed off. Surreptitiously, I exchanged parcels with him - I didn't fancy bills without scrap on.

Back home, I was having my tea when it suddenly started raining bills. Looking out, I saw John throwing bundles of them into the air.

"What's up John?" I asked, innocently.

"I've got the bills with no scrap on," he shouted. They're bloody useless."

"Don't be like that John," I said. "You can always ask for a bit of scrap."

John was fuming, but he calmed down eventually. I think we shared the good bills but can't be sure.

When we moved again we met up with Sam Lock, Jim Varey and Charlie Gaskin. We spent the greater part of that summer travelling together, mostly around Lincolnshire, Derbyshire, Nottinghamshire and Yorkshire.

Stopping near Grantham, a dozen or so of us teenagers had been to the pictures. We were on our way home when Peter Lock, Sam's son was taken ill with violent stomach pains. Rushed to hospital, he was found to have appendicitis and operated on immediately. The police came to move us on whilst Peter was in hospital, but we managed to persuade them to let us stay a week until he was discharged.

From Grantham, we moved to Bulwell where Charlie Gaskin parted company with us and moved to Mansfield in order to attend to some horses he had there. Sam Lock and my family travelled on to Dinnington Common, a Gypsy stopping place of many years standing.

Peter Lock, Dan Hockey (not his real name) and I went to Thurcroft cinema to see the Student Prince, Featuring Mario Lanza. Some of the Gypsy girls from Dinnington were there, this being the main attraction. Waiting for the 'bus home, Frank picked a fight with Peter over a bottle of beer. Peter was still convalescing from his appendix operation, so I intervened.

"Peter's in no fit state to fight," I told Dan. He's not long had an operation and he'll bust his stitches if he goes fighting. I'll fight you if you want to fight."

We fought on the spare ground opposite the 'bus stop and a crowd of Gypsy youngsters gathered round. After three or four minutes the 'bus came and our spectators left us to it, catching the 'bus for home. Peter stayed of course.

"Right!" said Dan. "That's it, I'm not fighting you here, there's nobody to see fair play and there's two of yus. I'll fight you back at home."

"Alright," I said. "If that's the way you want it we'll do that."

Having missed the 'bus we walked the two miles home and on arrival, Dan and I waited in the bushes whilst Peter brought Dan's brother to see fair play. Best was given after ten or fifteen minutes and we shook hands, but that was the end of our friendship.

In need of bills once again, I volunteered to bring some from the printer in Sutton-in-Ashfield, hoping I'd bump into Julie. Grove Road, where Julie's family were stopping was close to the printer's premises. Catching a 'bus to Sutton, I walked slowly passed Julie's trailer without seeing her. When I still didn't see her on the way back I called at the trailer with excuse that I was looking for Charlie Gaskin.

"Do you know where Charlie Gaskin's stopping Aunt?" I asked of Julie's mother, taking the opportunity to look inside the trailer when the door was opened. Apart from Julie's mother, Dolly, there were only two of the youngest children at home.

"Last I 'eard 'e was up by Skegby Sands," Dolly replied, looking at me quizzically. "Why? Is there summat wrong?

"Oh no, I just thought I'd call and see him," I lied.

"Would you like a cup of tea?" she asked. "Dennis won't be long."

I wasn't keen to see Dennis, Julie's father, so I hurriedly declined, claiming urgent business elsewhere.

Window shopping with Peter, in Worksop one day, I was looking in a hairdresser's window and on impulse decided I'd like to have my mop of unruly hair permed. After a lot of persuasion, Peter agreed to have his done too. Plucking up our courage, we went in and made an appointment for later that day. What a disaster! I had thought it would be all nice little soft curls. The reality I can only describe as a bush.

"How are we going to get rid of this?" Peter moaned, looking at his reflection in a shop window.

"I don't know," I said. "The woman said it'd last for weeks."

"I'm going to wash mine to death," Peter said. "I've got a head as big as a bucket." Peter washed his hair several times but it didn't improve matters much. My solution was to squash my hair under a trilby hat, which I wore constantly.

Shortly after that we moved near Sutton and Peter and I went into town, ostensibly to visit the fair that was there at the time. My real reason of course was the hope we'd meet Julie; and meet her we did. She had been on her way to the pictures but came with us to the fair instead. Again, I was struck by her beauty and personality and it was then I think that I fell in love with her.

We made a date to go to the cinema the following night, and on the way home, I resolved to ask her to be my steady girl. Julie had a boy friend at the time and I had been seeing a girl. In the cinema we both confessed to this and agreed to pack them in and 'go out together as the current phrase would have it. From that day on, Julie and I were together on every possibly occasion.

We were watching the picture when a woman sitting behind us tapped me on the shoulder.

"Would you mind removing your hat?" she requested politely. I complied, and my hair released from its constraint, shot up like a guardsman's busby.

"Oh! For goodness sake, put it back on," said the woman in alarm. Laughing, I obliged.

* * * * *

Jacksdale was our next stopping place. This was on a narrow strip of land between the road and the pit spoil heap. Wet weather made it very muddy and should someone complain of muddy conditions in some other camp, the stock reply was, 'well it's not as bad as Jacksdale'.

During the time we were there, many Gypsy families used the camp. It was unlicensed and belonged to a Brian Levers who collected five shillings (twenty five pence) rent per week from each family. Families on the camp included: Evans, Taylors, Prices, Braddocks, Locks, Vareys, Finneys, Ayres and ourselves.

John Ayres and I had a few weeks working together and did quite well. On one occasion, we bought a huge 4x4 lorry from a firm in Stavely that repaired railway waggons. Towing it back, we'd got as far as the crossroads on the A616 near Eckington when the front wheel bearing collapsed. We had oxy-acetylene cutting gear with us on our lorry and decided our best option was to cut the 4x4 up where it stood. One of us would be cutting whilst the other directed traffic around us. We were lucky to complete the job without attracting the attention of the police.

Julie's father was drinking heavily and in his cups was often violent and argumentative. Many's the times I've met Julie to find her bruised and bleeding after a beating from her father. Dennis would come home from the pub and start an argument with his wife. Julie would fly to her mother's defence and take the consequences.

Several times Julie left home to stay with us for a few days, sleeping with my mother whilst dad moved into the tent with me. Sometimes when we met, Julie would be minding her younger brother David and sister Star. We'd take them with us. Perhaps just for a walk, or occasionally for a meal. At other times, Julie would bring them to where we were stopping and we'd spend the day together.

Scrap collecting with dad, in Allestree near Derby, I spotted a caravan for sale. "That's a nice little trailer Dad," I said. "Do you think we could buy it?"

"Go an' ask what they want for it," Dad replied. "If it's not too much we pick your Mam up and see if she likes it."

Mother had been dropped off to hawk Ripley and we had arranged to collect her on the way home.

Enquiries proved the price of the caravan reasonably so we found Mother and with her approval bought it after a bit of haggling and towed it home. An Eccles Alert, it was a fairly modern van for the times and the envy of our friends. The cooker and lights ran on Calor gas, a new concept to us, and Mother was afraid of it. Several days elapsed before we persuaded her to try it. When she did however she seemed quite pleased with it and talking with friends, was wont to say, 'I'll just go and put the gas on for a cup of tea.'

Cousin Jimmy Finney came to live with us for a while. He bought an old, all white pony he called Tumbleweed to go scrap collecting with. Saddle backed, narrow chested, thin and lame on one front leg, it really was a pathetic animal.

"It's no use," he said one day. "I'm going to chop Tumbleweed away. I don't care what I chop for but he's got to go."

"What's made your mind up all of a sudden?" I asked.

"I'm sick of him," said Jim. "He's got a top speed of two miles an hour and if I get more than two hundredweight on the cart I have to help him pull it. Harry Bowers always has something in, I'll call today and see what I can do with him."

Harry lived in Mansfield and sometimes had a horse or two for sale.

"When you gets nearly there," one old Gypsy man advised Jim. "Tap your owd pony on 'is good leg just above 'is 'oof an' it'll make 'im walk sound for a bit."

"I'll try that," said Jim. "Do I have to hit him hard?"

"No, not at all," said the old man. "Just 'it 'im 'ard enough to make that leg as sore as t'other an' 'e won't know which one to favour."

Jim returned later that day without Tumbleweed.

"Did you chop him away then?" I asked.

"Yes," said Jim, smiling. "I chopped him for a whip."

"For a whip? What goods a whip without a pony?" I asked in surprise.

"Well, I drew twelve pounds to chop," laughed Jim. "And I reckon that was about the price of him."

"Did you hit him on his good leg like you said you would?" I asked.

"I did," said Jim. "But not very hard 'cos I didn't want to hurt him. I only gave him a gentle tap an' he fell down in the shafts. I got him to his feet and patted him and said I was sorry. Then I went in a little shop and bought him a bun. He was all right after that."

"Was he still lame?" I said, smiling at the mental picture of Jim apologising to his pony and feeding it a bun.

"He was just the same as always," Jim sighed.

"What made you chop for a whip?" I queried.

"Harry had no ponies in," said Jim. But he said he'd have one or two in a few days, so I left my cart with him until I find something to pull it."

Jim asked me to help him learn how to write his name, which I did, printing it in block capitals for him to copy. Two or three days later he proudly showed me how well he could do it. Taking the scrap of paper he handed me, I read, FIMMY JINNEY.

Moving to Cheadle in the Potteries, I bought two old 'buses for scrap. Made of aluminium, they were quite a good buy. The farmer I bought them from had them full of chickens.

"I'll be clearing them all out in a months time," the farmer told me. "You can have them then."

During that month the price of scrap aluminium fell through the floor. When we finally broke the 'buses up we made just seven pounds profit, and that for five days hard work. Well they say you can't win 'em all.

Julie came to stay with us for a couple of weeks - her dad had been up to his old tricks again. We received a letter, delivered to the post office where we collected our mail, threatening legal action if she didn't return, and Julie, being under age, had to go.

Towards the end of the year, we pulled in a little abandoned orchard in Eastwood, Notts - the Eastwood where D.H.Lawrence had once lived. Stopping with us was Charlie Gaskin, Snuffy Kennet, (not his real name) and Sam Lock.

I was working with Charlie buying old cars for scrap. Petrol was on ration at the time but when we bought an old car, we often got the petrol coupons with it. Coupons for private cars differed from those for a commercial vehicle and garages were not supposed to put petrol into a commercial vehicle in exchange for private car coupons, but none refused us. Consequently, we were never short of fuel.

There was a little mound of earth in the orchard and Charlie and I heaped our scrap on top of that so that there would look to be more than there was. We then sent for

Hendersons, the scrap metal people from Bulwell, hoping to get a good price for it. Whilst we were waiting for the scrap man to arrive, Tom Varey, Jack's brother turned up.

"What are you going to do with the scrap?" He asked.

"We're waiting for Hendersons, they're sending a man out to buy it," Charlie told him.

"I'll buy it," Tom said. "How much do you want for it?"

"Well we've sent for the man now," Charlie replied, not really wanting to sell it to Tom.

"My money's as good as Hendersons," Tom persisted. "If they turn up while I'm loading it I'll sell it to them an' we'll split any profit. I can't say fairer than that can I? Come on now, put it on price."

Reluctantly, Charlie sold the scrap to Tom, knowing there looked to be much more than there was. In all fairness, the heap had been 'cocked up' to catch Hendersons, not Tom, But Tom had insisted. Tom caught me with a load of scrap at a later date so I reckon we ended up even.

I had a puncture in my lorry and the tube was ruined. Snuffy collected scrap rubber and had a heap of old tyres and tubes by his trailer.

"Can I have a look for an old 32x6 tube in that pile Uncle?" I asked Snuffy.

"Course you can son," he said. "There'll be one in there somewhere."

"Got one. Thanks Snuffy," I said, after a short search. I was walking away with my prize when Snuffy called me back.

"That'll be ten bob," (fifty pence) he said, holding out his hand. I was amazed, I had expected to be given the tube, as I would have given it to him had the situation been reversed. I paid him and walked away without a word.

A week or so later, Charlie and I were cutting a car up when Snuffy walked across. "'Ow much is them owd wheels Charlie?" Snuffy asked. "I've got a man for them. I reckon I could swap them for a good load of scrap tyres. What do you want for 'em then."

Charlie, who knew about the incident with the tube, motioned in my direction.

"You'd better ask him," he grinned. "He's the boss today."

Snuffy looked at me questioningly.

"I'll take a fiver for them," I said. The going rate would have been about two pounds. It was Snuffy's turn to walk away.

"Thanks Charlie," I said, when Snuffy had gone.

"Serve the greedy old so and so right," said Charlie. "Revenge is sweet." I had to agree.

* * * * *

Julie and I would meet most evenings, either she would come to me or I to her, so when she failed to arrive four days on the run, I knew something was wrong. With not a little trepidation, I decided to pay her a visit at home. Wearing my best and only suit I caught the 'bus to Sutton, turning over in my mind what I would say to her parents when I got there. Thankfully, they had gone to the pictures when I arrived. Julie was in bed; ill with a kidney infection I believe she said. Her younger siblings, Susan, Geraline, Star, Dennis and David were there. Elder sister May was out.

Relieved that her father was at the cinema and not the pub, I chatted to Julie and waited anxiously for her parents to return. I didn't want to leave before they got back because I didn't want them thinking I'd called surreptitiously.

Aunt Dolly, Julie's mother came up the steps first.

"We've got a visitor Dennis," she warned, seeing me in the dim light of the candle.

"What do you want?" Dennis asked, coming in behind his wife.

"I just called to see how Julie was Uncle," I explained.

"Hmm," said Dennis, un-committedly.

"I was just going?" I said, standing up. Then turning to Julie, "I'll see you soon then." And I kissed her before brushing passed her parents and quickly making my exit, with a cheery, "Good night all."

Once again we moved to the Potteries and Julie and I kept in touch by 'phone. Public telephones then had a button 'A' and a button 'B', and if your call was connected, button 'A' was pressed, releasing the coins into the holding box. Should a call be unsuccessful, pressing button 'B' returned your money. All long distance, or trunk calls as they were termed, had to be connected by the operator and when the money had been used she would break in and say, 'Your time is up caller. Do you wish to pay for further time?'

Julie and I talked for ages, a two-hour stint being about average. At first the operator would break in regularly and ask for further payment, but after a few nights, we could talk as long as we wanted without having to pay more than the initial charge. I suspect the operators were listening in and either had a soft spot for lovers, or they enjoyed our conversation. Whatever the reason, it suited us and we took full advantage of it. I can still remember the number of Julie's telephone kiosk, Sutton 687 and I apologise to the queues of people that came to either box and waited for ages before giving up in disgust and stalking away.

Doodles Gaskin had married May, Julie's elder sister and was working with her father Dennis. They had moved from Grove Road to a piece of derelict land in Shirebrook. I ran into them now and then. Often they would both have had a drink or two - their normal days work usually started with a session in the pub. On one such occasion they were coming out of the Greyhound pub in Skegby as I was passing with my lorry, and Dennis flagged me down. We were stopping down Buttery Lane, Skegby, and Julie was once again staying with us.

"Is that wench of mine at your place?" Dennis asked. Knowing full well she was.

"Yes she is Uncle, I admitted. "Why?"

"I want her back home today," said Dennis. "If not there'll be trouble. Tell her will you?"

"What for?" I replied, surprised at my own audacity. "So that you can knock her about again? She can stop there as long as she wants."

Dennis's eyes bulged, but before he could say more, Doodles intervened. "Come on Dennis," he said, taking him by the arm. "Leave it for now." Leading him to their lorry, he helped him in and they drove off, much to my relief.

A couple of months or so later we were again stopping at Jacksdale and Julie was back at home. I was sitting cross-legged on the ground, cleaning some aluminium when to my surprise, I saw Dennis walking towards me. Not knowing what to expect, I stood up to greet him.

"Hello Uncle Dennis," I said. "What brings you this way?"

"My lorry's broke down," he explained. "Just up the road, and I've just maced a load of scrap. I could do with a bit of a tow to get me away from there." (To mace anything was to obtain it with promise of payment later, and Dennis was an expert.)

"Right!" I said, opening my lorry door for him. "Get in and we'll go and move it." Doodles was waiting with the broken down lorry when we got there.

"It's petrol trouble," he said. Wiping his oily hands on a bit of rag that seemed almost as oily, he went on. "Let's get it away from here. Tow us onto the car park behind the Butcher's Arms on the Alfreton road. We'll try and fix it there."

Dennis's Lorry was an old bull-nosed Morris and was heavily laden. I towed it to the pub with some difficulty - my clutch started to slip. Once there, Doodles removed the carburettor from the lorry and took it into the pub to clean it, ignoring the protestations of the publican, who complained that he was stinking the place out with petrol fumes.

Half an hour and a couple of pints later, the lorry was fixed and Dennis and Doodles went on their way. Driving home, I thought that Dennis was beginning to accept the inevitable, and as was his wont, making the most of it.

This view was re-enforced when a few weeks later Dennis again visited Jacksdale. After exchanging a few pleasantries, he came to the purpose of his visit.

"We've got to shift," he began, "And I've got no towbar on my lorry. I wondered if you'd move my trailers for me?"

"Where to?" I asked, cautiously.

"Well, on to here of would be best I suppose," he said.

"Course I will," I replied, secretly delighted at the prospect of Julie living on the same camp. "When do you want me?

"About ten in the morning if that's all right," he said. "Doodles is coming here as well, but he can move his own waggon. I've just got a puncture to mend on one trailer and I should be ready by ten."

"I'll be there," I said. And I was.

Jacksdale was quite full at this time. Apart from Dennis, Doodles and my family, other residents I remember were: John Ayres, Charlie Gaskin, Hope Price, Jack Taylor, Grandad Vitus Finney, Sam Lock, Jesse Evans, Bob Braddock and Aunt Louie Varey - her husband Jack being inside at the time.

Dennis and Doodles bought a lot of scrap from a garage and Dennis's lorry not being up to the job of moving it they asked me if I would like to stand in with it and move it with my lorry. This I did, and worked with them for a while after that, but I couldn't get used to their habit of calling at the pub before getting down to some work each day. Mind you, this method worked for them. I remember one time when Dennis had called at a garage that had a lot of scrap but had been unable to buy it.

"Let's call in the kitchimer (pub) for a livner," (beer) he said, not unexpectedly.

"Where to now?" I asked on leaving the pub a couple of hours later.

"Back to that garage," said Dennis.

"But he won't sell his scrap," I protested.

"He will," said Dennis. And he did.

Aunt Lina and my mother called me into the trailer one day.

"Do you intend to marry Julie?" Lina asked, when I entered the trailer.

"Yes! Of course I do," I replied, surprised at the question.

"You can do better you know," Mother chipped in.

"I don't think so," I said, annoyed. "And anyhow, I don't want to. I love Julie and we're going to be married."

"Her Mam and Dad won't give consent," Aunt Lina pointed out.

"That's my problem," I replied, walking out.

Julie and I had already talked about running away together if consent was not forthcoming. I didn't tell Julie of this conversation. I didn't see any point in hurting her feelings.

Jimmy Finney bought an old ten-hundredweight van. It was difficult to start in a morning, and one day, when he had been trying to start it without success for fifteen minutes or so, he asked if I'd give him a tow.

"Course I will." I said. "Get a chain on your van and I'll bring my lorry over." Tying the other end of the chain to my tow bar, I gently pulled his van onto the road. "Go on a bit faster?" Jim shouted. "It'll need a good snatch to get it going."

"Blow your horn when it starts," I told Jim. "And I'll know to stop."

We hadn't gone more than a few yards when I heard Jim's horn sounding continuously. Looking in my mirror, I saw Jim's van doing little jumps, as though it was trying to skip. Mystified, I stopped and walked back to him.

"What's up? Is it going then?" I started to say. But then I saw Jim was doubled up with laughter. "Look at the wheels! Look at the wheels!" he squeaked. Hardly able to speak for laughing.

I looked. Now if Jim's motor was pointing north, his two front wheels were pointing east and west respectively, rather like Charlie Chaplin's feet.

"You must have tied the chain round the track rod Jim," I said.

"What's ever's a track rod?" Jim asked, gasping for breath.

Jim's laughter was contagious and we stood there laughing like two fools, bursting into another fit of laughter every time we glanced at the van wheels. With the van skipping merrily along, I slowly towed it the short distance back to the trailers.

Once on the camp, Jim crawled under the van to remove the track rod in order to straighten it.

"What do you thinks wrong with the engine Tom. Why won't it start?" said Jim from beneath the van.

"I don't know Jim. Perhaps you've got a couple of spark plugs missing," I ventured. Meaning that perhaps some of his plugs was fouled and misfiring.

"No," said Jim, emphatically. "That's not it. There should only be four and there is, I've counted them."

Jim, I'm sure, knew what I meant and was pulling my leg.

* * * * *

"Do you want a jukel Tom?" Jim asked, returning from hawking one day.

"What sort is it?" I asked. I was down to one running dog at the time, having had as

46

many as eight previously.

"I don't know, it looks a bit like a wolf to me," said Jim.

"Why does the owner want to get rid of it?" I asked, intrigued. "What's wrong with it?"

"It's killed all his chickens," said Jim with a smile.

"Come on, let's have a look at it," I decided. And off we went.

Rusty, as I called him, turned out to be an Alsation - Elkhound cross. His coat was so thick the heaviest of downpours failed to penetrate it. It gave him protection from the hardest of frosts, and the teeth of the many dogs with which he fought.

He ignored the many chickens he encountered running loose on the camps we stayed on. My guess was that he had been blamed for the work of a fox. He was never tied up whilst I had him except for a brief period in South Wales, where loose dogs were shot as a matter of course by the sheep farmers.

Rusty was an excellent guard and safe with children. I had him for many years, long after the birth of my youngest son, Joe, and at thirty shillings, (one pound fifty) must rate as one of my best buys.

One by one, the families drifted away from Jacksdale. Towards the end of September, with the exception of Julie's and my family, only Doodles, Sam Lock, Charlie Gaskin and Jim Varey were left. The camp was ankle deep in mud so the exodus was understandable.

Julie and I decided to 'put the banns in' at the parish church of St, Helen's, Selston. Telling no one of our plans, we walked to the church one Sunday afternoon and saw the vicar, Reverend Pearse. We discovered that 'the banns' had to be read out in church on three consecutive Sundays and the earliest date we could marry would be October 21st. Agreeing the date, we were given a consent form to be signed by Julie's parents and an appointment was made for us to go to the vicarage for a rehearsal.

Now came the problem of getting Dennis and Dolly's consent. I decided to tackle them separately, Dolly first. Picking a time when I thought Dennis was in a good mood - he was really as nice a man as you could wish to meet when he was sober - I approached Julie's mother.

"Good morning Aunt," I said, standing at the door of her trailer. "Can I have a word."?

"What is it?" she replied, carrying on with her cleaning.

"Me and Julie are getting rumied," (married) I said. "We've put the banns in, but we need you to sign this paper to give your consent."

Dolly stopped what she was doing and stood looking at me for what seemed ages. "You'd better see her father," she said at last.

"Oh, I'm going to ask him now," I replied. "I just wanted to ask you, if it's alright with him, is it alright with you?"

"If he signs, I'll sign," said Dolly, turning back to her cleaning.

'That was the easy part', I thought, going in search of Dennis. I spotted him sitting on a pile of old car tyres, smoking, and walked casually across. Handing him the consent form, I said. "Will you sign this for me Uncle Dennis?"

"Why? Whatever is it child?" he asked.

"It's for me and Julie to get married," I explained.

"Married!" he exclaimed. "I don't know about that. She's only a baby. You'd better see what her mother has to say about that."

"Oh, I've already asked Aunt Dolly," I said. "She said it's alright."

"That's it then," said Dennis. "If she says it's alright." Resting the paper on the bonnet of a scrap car, he signed without further ado.

"Thanks Uncle Dennis," I said, taking the precious piece of paper from him.

"When's this wedding to be then?" Dennis asked.

"In a fortnight," I told him. "At the little church up the road.

Julie's mother made her mark on the form when I told her Dennis had signed, and I was elated. Getting consent had worried me for some time; I would never have believed it would be so easy.

That weekend, Charlie Gaskin, Sam Lock and Jim Varey moved on, leaving Julie's family, my family and Doodles and May as the sole occupants of the camp. Four or five days before Julie and I were to be married, I drove to where they were stopping in Gypsy Lane, near Derby, to invite them all to the wedding, but they didn't come. Julie and I had very little money: in fact, on the day of the wedding I had eight pounds left. Our home to be was the eight-foot by eight-foot tent I slept in, and that was on loan from my parents.

Julie had a navy blue suit made at Burtons. The skirt had three box pleats back and front. My suit, also made at Burtons had box pleats in the back of the jacket, gauntlet cuffs, open seams and patch pockets - a common Gypsy style.

Came the morning of the wedding and I found I had no socks to wear. Julie and I drove in my lorry to Woolworth's in Sutton and waited for them to open in order to buy some. When we told the assistant we were getting married at ten-o-clock that morning she made us a present of the socks - the only wedding present we received.

Carnations for buttonholes had been ordered from an allotment holder I knew, pink for the bride and white for everyone else. Doodles made a big fuss, saying that he wanted a pink one. I was getting quite heated explaining that the pink one was for the bride, but he would have none of it. He had me going for some time before I realised he was winding me up.

I drove to the church in my lorry with my parents in the cab and Doodles and May riding on the back.

Leaving us at the church, Doodles then took my lorry back to collect the bride to be and her parents.

After the ceremony, we all piled into my lorry and adjourned to the Butchers Arms for a drink. We stayed 'till closing time and then, rather the worse for drink, it was back in the lorry and home.

That, then, was our wedding day.

Amelia Taylor,
Julie's granny

Dolly Booth,
Julie's mum

Tom's granny, Lizzie Finney with son Billy and daughter Lizzie

A very young Tom with his dad

Wagon Time.

First wagon: *a Bill Wright's wagon with Sam Lock, Louie on the horse, Peter on the running board and baby Ann with mum Lina.*

Second wagon: *thought to be an older model Bill Wright's wagon showing Sam and Annie McCready.*

Third wagon: *with Jim Varey.*

JULIE'S STORY

JULIE'S STORY

My father, Dennis Booth, was the youngest son of a Fred and Florrie Booth. He had two brothers, George and Mandy, and two sisters, Violet and Lizzie. George married my mother's sister, Mayfield.

Mother was a Taylor before her marriage. Her parents were Amelia and Silvester (Trout) Taylor.

Both my maternal grandparents had been married before and their combined offspring were said to exceed twenty. Those I know are: Henry, Noah, Silvester, Duval, Ezzy, Horace, (known as Mushy) Rueben, Nellie, Violet and Mayfield.

My earliest memories begin when I was about four years old. We were stopping in Friar's Yard, Burn Street, Sutton-in-Ashfield. I had a half sister May, born in May 1938. Mother had been pregnant with her when she married my father - much against the wishes of Father's family, I'm told.

Another child had been born in 1940, a girl. She only lived eight hours. Father made the coffin she was buried in out of an apple box begged from the local greengrocer.

I was born on the Christmas Eve of that year, in the open lot that was our home in Friar's Yard. It was usual for births to take place at home before the National Health Service came into being. Hospital charges were beyond many people's reach - the midwife was much cheaper.

I'm told Dad lay drunk on the waggon floor when the midwife came to deliver me. Ignoring his complaints, Nurse Hunt bundled him outside and ordered him to keep out of the way. This was just one of the many occasions Nurse Hunt attended my mother's confinements - her fee was half-a-crown (twelve and a half new pence).

Mother told me she was alarmed by my appearance when I was born. A membrane known as a widow's veil covered my face. Mother's sister Mayfield removed it, saying, "You should sell that to a seaman Dolly, they says them's lucky an' anybody what's got one will never drown."

My christening took place at Bourne, in Lincolnshire, in the June of '41, so we must have been travelling at the time.

Friars yard was a stopping place for many Gypsy families during the war years. Names of Gypsy families I remember are: Gaskin, Price, Woodward, Holmes, Newbury, Rook, Bowers, Gallagher, Winters, Eggerton, Walton, Moss, McGuire and Booth. Families came and went and the population of Friar's Yard was in a constant state of flux.

My parent's marriage was a stormy one to say the least. Father liked a drink and the drink made him argumentative. Many of the rows Father and Mother had were very violent. I first became aware of this around my fourth birthday. Most of the adults on the site had gone for a Christmas drink and May and I had been left in the care of an elderly relative, a Mrs. Eggerton, supposedly very deaf.

"Would you like a cup of tea my gels?" asked Mrs. Eggerton. To which we both nodded. On receiving the tea, I whispered to May. "I don't like this, it's like cat's piss."

55

Mrs. Eggerton reached over and took my cup from me, saying. "Give it 'ere them lass. That's the last you get from me."

I've since come to the conclusion that Mrs. Eggerton was only deaf when it suited her.

Put to bed in our waggon, May and I heard the adults returning from the pub. Mother and Father were arguing and, from the sound of it, fighting. A crowd gathered in front of the waggon, trying to calm them down. After a while they seemed to succeed and Mother came into the waggon with dad's sister Violet. Mother put the kettle on the stove to boil for tea. Kneeling by the front of the stove, she was lifting the boiling kettle in order to fill the teapot by the light of the fire when Dad lifted the sheet of the open lot.

"You f...ing bitch!" he shouted. "You was going to scald me with that, wasn't you?" Before Mother could speak, Dad leapt inside and kicked her in the mouth, knocking out two of her front teeth.

"You bastard!" Mother screamed, and flew at him. Aunt Violet was in the middle desperately trying to separate them.

There's not much room to hide in a waggon but May and I, terrified, squeezed ourselves as small as we could beneath the bottom bed. Eventually, Eddie Eggerton, Violet's husband, rescued us and took us to their waggon for the night. This was to set the pattern of our parents' married life. More of this anon.

Between the ages of four and five I was enrolled at the local infant's school, the Hillocks on Coxmoor Road. Several Gypsy children attended this school, as did my sister May and my cousin Laurel Booth. Laurel is the daughter of my dad's brother George.

Across the bottom of the school playground was a huge Anderson shelter. We would have an air raid drill during which we were made to wear the gas mask we always carried and run to the shelter. The shelter was buried in the ground and I hated going into this big dark hole.

Apart from that, I quite enjoyed school, especially the dinners. I attended this school for three or four month before the family left to travel Lincolnshire, but during the time I was there I managed to pick up the rudiments of reading.

Uncle George and Dad's parents accompanied us on this trip and we spent the summer travelling. Mother, Aunt May, cousins Louie and Dennis, and on occasion, Dad's mother would hawk the villages of Lincolnshire.

Aunt May had a little mare, Pansy, that would pull the trap they used. Their stock in trade was clothes pegs, wooden flowers, baskets, paper flowers and wooden skewers, all made at home. Making these items, and gathering the materials for them was the task of the menfolk and younger children. They also provided a shushi (rabbit) or two, or perhaps a kanengro (hare) or boshni (pheasant) and sometimes a hochiwichi (hedgehog) for the pot.

Many Gypsies regard Hochiwichi as a delicacy. They are not rolled in clay and baked, as many would have it, but can be boiled, pot roast, or best of all, cooked on a skewer over an open fire. First, the hedgehog had to be killed and to do this he had to be opened. Dad would put his foot on the hedgehog's back and rock it back and forth. Slowly the animal would unroll. A smart tap on the head with a stick killed it instantly and it was then thrown onto the fire for a few seconds. Removed from the fire, hochi then had his bristles shaved with a sharp peg-knife and his back opened to remove his entrails. 'A hedgehog carries his belly in his back,' Dad told me. When washed in salt water, hochi' was ready to cook.

Once, when Mother had cooked a hedgehog, she said, "'Ere you are Julie, I've saved the best bit for you, It'll last you all day." The 'best bit' turned out to be it's little kory (penis), as I found out later, much to my disgust and to shrieks of laughter from the other kids.

Sometimes Dad would raid a hen house for a chicken and a few eggs. We kids would take vegetables from the fields or potatoes from a potato hog. With this and the food Mother would beg whilst hawking, such as bacon, cheese, eggs, butter and home made jam, we didn't go short. These being the war years, and rationing very strict, all such additions to our diet were very welcome.

The Ministry of Food provided concentrated orange juice and cod-liver oil and malt combined, a treacle like substance, to families with children. Orange juice was nice but we didn't like the cod-liver oil and malt very much. It came in a large jar and we were told that a spoonful a day provided us with all the vitamins we needed to stay healthy. To ensure that we took it, Mother would put it in the cupboard and say, "Now children, I don't want you touching that, it's very special stuff to make people big and strong", knowing full well that as soon as her back was turned we'd each have a dip.

Tobacco was particularly hard to come by and as both my parents smoked, an opportunity to acquire some was never missed - often via the black market. The black-market was a kind of shady business that went on during the war. Dealers in black-market goods were called spivs. Most things in short supply they could obtain, from goodness knows where, selling them on at exorbitant prices to whoever would buy. This trade was illegal of course.

Should a pub or shop have a legal supply of tobacco to sell, it was often kept under the counter to be offered only to special customers. Dad however, could charm the sugar from your tea and would often wheedle a few cigarettes or a bit of 'baccy from the proprietor.

We never saw sugar or sweets, sweetening our tea or cocoa with Nestle's sweetened, condensed milk. Thick slices of bread, spread with Nestle's milk took the place of sweets. I couldn't eat it now, but then I considered it a treat.

Often, whilst travelling, my sister May, cousin Laurel and I would be sent to the nearest school, perhaps just for a couple of days. This usually happened when the menfolk were busy with some business or other that took them away for a day or so. School was looked upon as a safe place to leave us whilst the women hawked.

With the end of the war came the return of the horse fairs and sometimes our travels would take in one or two. Maybe Lee Gap, Barnby Dun, Brough, Boroughbridge or Appleby. We looked forward to these fairs, for there we'd meet up with friends, relatives and families whom we perhaps hadn't seen since the last fair.

Horse fairs were colourful events, with brightly painted waggons and carts, horses with coloured ribbons plaited into their manes and tails and everyone dressed in their best. Two old spinsters living in Sutton made our clothes. They knew how to make the dresses 'Gypsy fashion' and were known as the sewing sisters. Men also liked to dress up, corduroy trousers, plaid shirts and brown leather boots being favoured by many.

Most of the dealing would be done in the pub. Horses, dogs, waggons, carts, chickens, caged birds, gold rings and chains, nothing was sacred; almost anything could be bought if the price was right. Women sat round the fires dotted here and there, exchanging news and telling of things that had happened since last they met. Children would meet friends they had spent other happy times with and a good time was had by all.

When the pubs turned out, the menfolk would drift back to the waggons, often laden with bottles of beer for the women, plus a few more for themselves of course. Someone would strike up a tune with a fiddle or accordion and the singing and dancing would continue long into the night.

All good things come to an end they say and when the fair was over, the waggons would take to the road again. With many shouted goodbyes and much waving they would head off in a dozen different directions to resume their travels. To meet again maybe, somewhere, sometime.

Dad was exempt from military service on medical grounds. He was prone to epilepsy and considered unfit to serve. Some Gypsies avoided conscription by being constantly on the move. Stopping in a Lincolnshire lane on one occasion, I remember a Gypsy man running into camp holding his trousers up with one hand - he'd probably have been relieving himself behind the hedge.

"Muskeros! Muskeros! Gavo!" he shouted. (Police! Police! hide!) Many of the men in the camp took to their heels across the field out of sight of the lane. They hid in a ditch filled with water for the rest of that day and most of the following night. Military police came marching into camp almost before the men were out of sight.

"Where are your menfolk?" an officer demanded of the few old men that remained.

"There's only us," one of them replied.

"And what about you?" the officer said, pointing to my father.

"What about me?" said Dad.

"Why aren't you in the army?" The officer wanted to know.

"I'm exempt," said Dad, handing the officer his crumpled bit of paper.

The officer examined the document minutely before handing it back.

Whilst this was going on the other soldiers were searching everywhere, in waggons and tents, under canvas covers and in any other place they thought might conceal a man. Satisfied at last, they moved off, promising to return at a later date. Dad, along with the older men and the women yoked the horses and moved at first light next morning - the sodden young men rejoining the waggons along the way.

*   *   *   *   *

Autumn of the year found us making our way back to Friar's Yard for the winter. Mother and her Sister Mayfield were both in an advanced stage of pregnancy. A settled stopping place was desirable for the births and Friar's Yard was the usual choice. Before we reached there however, Mother went into labour. We had got as far as Warsop in Nottinghamshire and camp had been made in Sookholm Lane, just four or

58

five mile from Sutton. It was there that my sister Geraline was born.

Grandad Fred was taken ill in Sookholm Lane and as soon as we could, we completed the journey to Friar's Yard. Shortly after reaching the yard, Grandad died. He is buried in the cemetery of St. Mary's Church, Sutton.

Aunt Mayfield's baby, Silvester, was born about the same time as my sister Geraline was, but I don't remember anything of the birth.

In the spring of '45, Uncle George and family moved away. We followed a few weeks later to join them at Whitwell, near Worksop where Mother and her sister Mayfield were taken ill. Mother had pneumonia and was taken to Kilton Hospital, Worksop. Aunt Mayfield refused to be admitted. Whilst in Kilton Hill Mother received the devastating news that her sister Mayfield had died. I'm not sure of the cause of her death. Some have told me it was pneumonia and others lockjaw. Her death was a terrible blow to the family. She was only 38 and left four children, the youngest just a few months old.

We all moved back to Friar's Yard again and Aunt Mayfield was buried in Sutton cemetery, near Grandad. Cousin Louie was about fifteen years old. She took on the job of looking after the younger children and running the home after her mother's death. Uncle George moved on and we didn't see the family for a while.

Over the next couple of years, we travelled with my maternal grandparents, Dad's sister Violet, Tommy Gaskin and many other Gypsy families, including Jimmy Berry. Jimmy was well known for his skill in painting waggons. An example of his work can be seen in the Castle Museum, York. In later years, he was to beat the panel on TV's 'What's my line?' the panel failing to guess his occupation as a Gypsy waggon painter. Dad was also a dab hand at painting waggons and plied this trade up and down the country painting waggons for many Gypsies. At one time, there was talk of Dad and Jimmy joining forces, but Dad was too fond of the drink to do it full time.

Suddenly, it was V.E.Day. War hadn't had much effect on us as children. Gas masks, soldiers, rationing, and air-raid sirens were just a part of everyday life. V.E.Day however is a vivid memory. I would be nearly five. We were stopping in a Lincolnshire lane somewhere, along with Aunt Violet, Mother's parents, some of Mother's brothers and one or two other Gypsy families.

Everybody was celebrating in the local village. I can recall sitting outside the pub on a dray (four-wheeled horse drawn cart) with about a dozen Gypsy children. Mam's brother Reuben was left outside to look after the horses and us. There were a good many carts drawn up at the pub and all the Gypsy men and women were inside having a real old knees up. Bells were ringing, sirens sounding, people singing, dogs barking, children laughing and crying, everybody enjoying themselves - a happy bedlam.

When the last of the revellers had been ejected from the pub, a motley band of Gypsies made their way back to the waggons to continue the celebrations. Those that could not stand were thrown onto the carts, along with several crates of whatever alcohol could be acquired. Those that were able, drove the horses and collected firewood along the way, including a few farmer's gates and fence posts. At the camp, a huge fire was built and celebrations went on long into the night.

Back at Friar's Yard, we learned that it was to be closed to make way for a new estate of council houses and Gypsy families were looking for alternative winter accommodation.

Dad's mother had been found a stopping place in Glover's Yard, a small plot down Grove Road, Sutton-in-Ashfield. There was two other small yards down Grove Road used by Gypsy families and Ben Wooley, a local scrap merchant, also opened a stopping place for Gypsies down Carsic Lane, Sutton.

When we left Friar's yard for the last time, we were on the road for a year before returning to pull in Glover's Yard for the bad winter of 1947. Uncle George had established himself at Stairfoot, near Barnsley, setting himself up in the scrap metal business. This proved a very successful venture for him and continues to be so to this day. George now lives in a bungalow he had built in Shafton, near Barnsley.

Dad was drinking heavily and he and mother had another of their rows. When father poured paraffin over Mam and tried to light it with a match, Uncle George, who was visiting his mother at the time, intervened. Knocking the matches from Dad's hand, George managed to calm Dad down and a potential disaster was averted.

We moved as soon as the weather allowed, pulling onto a piece of wasteland in Brigg Street, just half a mile or so away. Brother Dennis was born there in the early hours of February 19th, - a cold and snowy night - the first son to be born to a very proud dad whose previous children had all been girls.

Nurse Hunt was attending to Mother and Geraline was asleep in the bottom bed. Father had made a huge fire near the wall that separated the wasteland from the houses, and May, Dad and myself, were huddled round it.

Suddenly a woman's face appeared over the wall - she must have been standing on something because the wall was about six feet high.

"Whatever do you think your doing lighting that fire at this time of night?" she enquired of Father.

"My wife's in labour Missus," Dad told her. "And the midwife's with her. I've built this fire to try and keep these two warm. It's a bad 'owd night Lady."

"It's too bad a night for them kids to be out," said the woman, mollified. "Why don't you bring them round to my house? They can have warm and a bit of something to eat."

"Thank you Missus, that's very good of you," Dad accepted gratefully.

"They can stop a couple of days 'till you get your troubles over if you want," the woman told Dad when he took us round. "They can sleep with my two daughters, Eileen and Nancy. They're about the same age as your two."

"Thank you Missus. That's very good of you," Dad said again. With that he went back to his vigil by the fire and we were ushered into the woman's kitchen, where we were given a cup of cocoa before being packed off to bed with the two daughters.

Next morning we were given toast and tea, but the tea was sweetened with treacle and I couldn't drink mine. The lady was very kind to us. Her daughter Nancy couldn't speak properly and wasn't able to pronounce my name. She would call me Tulip and I thought it very amusing.

During the next month or so, Ambrose Booth, Dad's nephew, taught Dad to drive and Dad bought an old car. The car had a dickey seat at the back, where the boot is on a modern car, and we children loved to ride in it.

We left Brigg Street in the spring, towing the waggon with the car. That year Dad did a bit of dealing as usual and we ended the summer back in Sutton with two horses and another waggon, the car having been swapped away.

Sutton council had provided a stopping place for Gypsies called the New Site. Built on a piece of land known as the Sheepwash, this is where we stopped that winter. Mother's parents were on the site, along with Dad's sister Violet, various Gaskins, some Bells, Woodwards, Lees, Newburys, Hope Price and a man called Jimmy Gill.

Jimmy Gill had no legs and would get around on a little cart he'd made himself from a set of old 'pram wheels. He was very strong, and could launch himself from the ground with his arms and jump onto his waggon front-board, some four or five feet high.

Another character on the site, and one of Dad's drinking partners was Fred Smith, or 'Mansfield Dealer' to his Gypsy friends. I'm told he acquired the nickname because of a series of notable deals he was involved in during one of his visits to Mansfield. "He'll chop for 'owt," Dad said of him.

Dad decided it was time we went into motors and trailers. "Everybody's getting 'em," he said. "Horses and waggons are a thing of the past."

I'd be about nine years old at the time and looked forward excitedly to this new way of life. Being handy with his hands, Dad bought the back off an old bread van to convert into a 'Whoopy trailer'. This was a type of home made trailer favoured by many Gypsy families getting out of horses and waggons, mainly because it was the cheapest way to make the transition. Just a square box on wheels really, with a waggon interior fitted. Having two side windows as opposed to a bow topped waggons one little back window. They were quite comfortable to live in and many thought an improvement on the horse drawn waggon.

Our 'Whoopy' completed, Dad sold our waggon to Old Hope Price. We children could not have foreseen how this change of accommodation would change our way of life. From a nomadic existence, we changed to an almost stationary way of life, and one that I came to hate.

From a child's point of view, one of the main disadvantages of being settled was that all the children on the site were obliged to attend school. Sister May, found this particularly galling. She was then thirteen years old and used to hawking with her mother. School put paid to that.

I grasped every opportunity to go hawking with my maternal grandmother, and accompanying her most Saturdays and occasionally sneaking the odd day off school. Granny Amelia drove a small two-wheeled cart pulled by a little mare called Grasni - which means mare in Romanies. She sold brushes of every description, along with wooden flowers, pegs and baskets all made by Grandad Trout. Grandad Trout made my first hawking basket, and I thought myself quite grown up as I accompanied Granny or my mother to the doors and listened to their patter.

Whilst hawking, Granny would carry an assortment of her wares in a huge square basket hung on her arm. In her free hand, she always carried a hand-brush.

"What's the little brush for Granny?" I asked one day.

"It's for them bad ol' jukles, my gel," she said with a smile. "A crack across the nose with that when they comes a worryin' yer, soon makes 'em change their minds."

Despite having to go to school, living on the site did have some advantages. Water was on tap; there was always plenty of company and the Gypsy way of life continued for the most part. Food was still cooked on open fires and the menfolk would still go rabbiting and coursing hares, though they would probably have to hunt further afield.

Behind the site was a huge pond known as The Dam, and rowing boats could be hired there. One Sunday afternoon, Dad was coming home - in company with several of his drinking cronies from the site - after a session in the pub. Passing The Dam, someone impulsively suggested they hire a couple of boats. They did and during the horseplay that followed a concerted attempt was made to throw Dad overboard. Had they succeeded, Dad would surely have drowned, he was a non-swimmer and The Dam was very deep.

I had been given a little dog that I called Kushti (good). When she broke her two front legs in the joint between the waggon shafts and the lock, Dad put her in a bag and threw her into The Dam and I cried for days. He could be a very cruel man where animals were concerned. The Dam also became the repository for Granddad's gold pocket watch, thrown in by Father - I never knew why.

Behind The Dam was an area known as The Lawn. Here could be found a children's boating pool, swings, a slide, a roundabout, tennis courts and bowling greens. With a tuck shop and toilets, it was a magical playground for children and we spent many happy hours there.

Near the site was a very tall chimney, known as Fenchurch's Chimney and a steel ladder ran from bottom to top. During a game of dare, a shilling was offered to any child who would climb the chimney and touch the lightening conductor spike on the top. I accepted the challenge, much to sister May's horror. She ran home screaming for Dad as I started to climb. I was about half way up when Dad arrived with a tribe of Gypsies from the camp.

"Come down here now, you daft little bastard," Dad roared at the top of his voice. "I'll teach you to go climbing when I get 'old of you. Get down now."

"Kek (no) don't trash (frighten) 'er Dennis," I heard Mother say. "Leave 'er come down of 'er own accord. You'll 'ave 'er fallin'".

Determined to earn my shilling, I ignored the shouts and threats and carried on touch the spike. Climbing gingerly down, I was pounced upon by Mother as soon as I reach the ground. She dragged me home and gave me a good hiding on the way with an aluminium saucepan she happened to be holding. That little escapade was a talking point amongst the site residents for some days and despite my bruises, I was proud of myself. Although the dare was repeated several times, no one else took up the challenge.

We had been on the site some months when Uncle George came on one of his regular visits.

"How's business?" he asked Dad as they sat round the outside fire.

"I'm finding it a bit quite at the moment," Dad admitted. "There doesn't seem to be much money about to tell the truth."

"Why don't you come to work with me for a bit?" George offered. "I've plenty on and I could do with a bit of a hand."

"If that's the case I will. I could do with a change anyway, I've seen enough of Sutton for a bit."

Dad was delighted to accept George's offer and we moved to Stairfoot near Barnsley the very next day. May and I were pleased to see Cousin Laurel again and it was nice to have the company of a different group of Gypsy children. Mother was not so pleased. Stairfoot was just another site and Mother didn't like sites and was always complaining about stopping in one place too long. But times were changing. Many of the men were collecting scrap metal, and some had regular suppliers. Consequently, they were not inclined to move about so much. Once again, I was sent to school, much to my dismay. Laurel and May, being older, were allowed to go hawking.

* * * * *

Working with Uncle George, Dad had money in his pocket again and was drinking every night with the men from the camp. Mother was unhappy. Apart from Dad's drinking, Stairfoot was not a pleasant camp. Over crowded and dirty, it was built alongside an old railway line. Without electricity or toilets, the only amenity was a solitary water tap near the gate. This then was home to dozens of Gypsy families, and quite a few gaujos trying to be Gypsies.

Filling a can with water one day, I saw a couple walk onto the camp pushing a pram containing their baby son and all their worldly possessions. Uncle George was dealing in used Anderson Shelters - he had a contract to supply them to the local pits, where they were used to shore up the roofs. Seeing that the couple were homeless, George and some of the Gypsy men got together and built up an extra large Anderson Shelter for the them. George also gave the man a job for a while to help him out.

Sometimes, May, Laurel and I would build a fire outside of an evening. This would attract the other boys and girls and we would all sit and talk of this and that. One evening the talk came round to ghost stories and some of them were quite awesome. Each teller would insist that their stories were true and that they had witnessed them personally. By the end of the evening, I was terrified. So much so that I didn't dare leave the light of the fire to go home, unless May or Laurel held my hand.

"Go an' see if Old Letty's got a tuvlo (cigarette) spare will you?" Mother asked, one evening. "I'm dying for a fag and your dad won't be back from the pub for hours. Tell 'er I'll send 'er one back as soon as 'e gets 'ome."

Now Letty had been the subject of one of the ghost stories a few evenings before.

"Sold 'er soul to the Mullo (Devil) 'er 'as," one of the boys had said. "Comes an visits 'er 'e does, any time 'e likes. I wouldn't go over there at night for a gold pig."

Letty's old waggon was pulled over by a clump of trees we called the elder wood, and the thought of venturing there on my own filled me with terror. Consequently, I rounded up half a dozen of the Gypsy girls to accompany me on my errand.

"Come on up, come up," the old woman invited when we explained our missic her waggon steps. No one wanted to be left outside alone, so we all squeezed in waggon whilst Letty rummaged in her bag for her cigarettes. Suddenly, a black emerged from beneath the waggon bed.

"It's the Mullo!" Laurel screamed, "It's the Mullo! Let me out."

With one accord, we made for the door. In a melee of arms and legs, w shouting and screaming bunch at the foot of the old woman's steps. Whe

63

feet, I was the only one left and the old woman was peering at me anxiously.

"Are you all right my gel?" Letty enquired. "Did my old jukel trash you? He's very old you know an' he wunner 'urt you. 'Ere my lass, you'd better tek this to your mam." With that Letty handed me the cigarette and I was off.

When I told my mother how the others had left me alone with Old Letty and the Devil, Mother laughed. "Don't be so silly wench," she chided. I've known that Old Letty for years, she's just a lonely old woman who wouldn't 'urt a fly, an' that old jukel of 'ers is as 'armless as she is. Get off with you lass and don't be a dinglo." For all that, I wouldn't go near Old Letty's place again. Thinking of it now brings a smile to my face and I hope the old lady wasn't offended by our foolishness.

We had been on Stairfoot perhaps three or four months when my parents had a violent row, probably brought on by my father's constant drinking. The upshot was that we left the camp next morning. Dad's niece Florrie, and her husband Fred, made the move with us. Fred and Florrie still had horses and a waggon whilst we had a big old car of some sort and the 'whoopy' Dad had made. I'm not sure where we went but we ended up at Pilsley, near Tibshelf, in Derbyshire a few months later.

May and I were hawking with cousin Florrie and my mother every day. Dad would stay at home to mind the younger children, Dennis and Geraline. We were camped in a field behind a farm, courtesy of the farmer and were very content. On occasion, we visited the local cinema and May and I made friends of some gaujo girls. They gave us books and toys, rare commodities in our family.

Fred and Florrie moved after a while, and we moved back to Sutton. The New Site had been closed we found, and some of the residents scattered to various little yards around Sutton. Many had moved onto a field owned by a scrap merchant called Ben Wooley, whilst a few had gone into houses, having been offered a key by the council when the New Site was closed.

Dad found a little yard for us down Grove Road, almost opposite the yard where his mother Florrie lived. This I believe was the worst place we could have chosen to stop. Grannie Florrie had a great influence on Father, taking his side in any argument he had with Mother, and giving him money for drink when he was short. We did move again for a short time, but Mother was pregnant again and we returned to Grove Road, where my sister Susan was born.

Lias and Nellie Winter, an old Gypsy couple, lived in one of the little yards down Grove Road. They had two sons, the eldest married and travelling, and young Lias, who lived at home. Old Lias was as fond of a drink as was my dad and was one of dad's drinking mates. Inevitably, this was the cause of friction between Lias and Nellie.

Although more often drunk than sober, when he wasn't drinking, Dad was a different person. A nicer man you could not wish to meet. People who only knew him sober could not believe how violent he could be in drink. Mother was probably the instigator of many of their rows. She would start shouting and reprimanding him when he came home drunk, knowing full well what the outcome would be.

Should Dad come home from the pub in a good mood, and if Mother didn't provoke him, he would oft times regale us with stories of things he'd done in the past. He'd tell of deals he'd had, good and bad, amusing incidents that had happened and also of the characters he'd met, many of whom he'd borrowed a few pounds from, never to be repaid.

One such was a pork butcher who had a shop in Sutton. Apparently, Dad had managed to tap him for a fiver at some time. Wending his way home from the Blue Bell in Sutton one day, Dad happened to meet up with this butcher.

"Well, Hello Dennis," he said. "It's been a long while since you was in my shop. Where have you been keeping yourself? Don't you think it's about time you paid off your debts? I could do with that fiver you owe me."

"Sorry owd lad," Dad replied. "I haven't got it, and I don't know that I should give it to you if I had. You don't pay owd debts wi' new brass yer know. Anyhow, I'm skint, and you can't get feathers off a cat."

"No, but I can get skin from bone," snarled the irate butcher. "And I'll have some from you if I don't get my money back." That I think was probably the end of that friendship.

Then there was the time that Dad and Lias Winter got roaring drunk together. Lias couldn't stand at all. Dad wasn't much better, but he borrowed a wheelbarrow from the publican to wheel Lias home in. Having got Lias into the barrow with the help of the barman, they set off for home, with Lias singing at the top of his voice and Dad weaving from one side of the road to the other. The half-mile journey through Sutton took about an hour. How they made it without being stopped by the police or getting run over I'll never know.

Sometimes Dad would be off the beer for a couple of weeks or so. He would be pleasant and cheerful and these would be good times for all the family. We all knew, though, that it wouldn't last and that Dad would soon be back on the booze.

Nellie was a good friend of Mother's, two people in the same boat I suppose. Most evenings, Nellie would visit Mother for a chat and on Sundays, they would often go to the pictures together. Nellie's father, Old Fred Moss, lived in a big waggon in Glover's Yard, near my granny. This enabled Nellie to keep an eye on his well-being. Fred was quite old, maybe seventy or so.

Nellie being with my mam during her confinement caused quite a stir in my family. You see, Nellie was cross-eyed, and when baby Susan was born, she had a cast in one eye. Father swore it was because Nellie had been the first to see and hold the baby, that she was so afflicted. Despite Mother's protests, Nellie was forbidden to visit our trailer again. She did, but only when Dad was out.

When Old Fred died, Nellie cleared out his old waggon and sold it to Punch Bancroft, another of Dad's drinking pals. Punch kept a few horses, mainly to hire out for the gaujos to ride. He kept his horses tethered on a piece of wasteland known locally as The Rec, short for recreation ground I suppose. The Rec was about half a mile from Grove Road and if I was about when Punch wanted a horse fetching for someone to ride, I would go. This earned me the princely sum of two shillings, (ten pence) but I did learn to ride, albeit after falling off a few times.

May sometimes came with me to fetch Punch's horses, and when she did, we would force his hand for an extra two shillings. We were very grateful for any extra money we earned like this. Two shillings paid for a night out at the pictures. Any other money we earned was given to Mother for food.

Punch once offered to sell us a horse and flat cart he'd bought cheap from Mansfield horse fair. May and I were delighted at the thought of a turnout of our own. The asking price of twenty-five pounds was a lot of money in those days, but we were confident we could soon earn it if we went old stuffing (scrap collecting) with the turnout. However, Punch declined to sell on a pay as you earn basis and when we approached Dad for a loan, he refused point blank. I couldn't understand Dad's refusal, he was earning good money at the time, old stuffing was good and we'd soon have paid him back. Lots of Gypsy boys and girls were doing well old stuffing. A lost opportunity, we thought.

School could not be avoided. Any child between the ages of five and fifteen could be taken into care if they didn't receive full time education. Although May, Geraline and I made many good friends amongst the gaujo community, and I remember with pleasure the many adventures I shared with them, school was still a bind. When Uncle George visited Grannie Florrie, as he did from time to time, he would bring Cousin Laurel with him. Whilst there she would attend school with us, making the irritation more bearable.

I'd be about thirteen when brother David was born. May had left school and used to mind the younger ones when Mam and Dad went hawking. Saturdays and holidays would find me in the role of baby-sitter, allowing May to go hawking with Mother. Dad was earning good money, every penny of which was spent in the pub. Had he been a more responsible father. we would have been quite well off, by Gypsy standards anyway.

I was growing up pretty quickly now and missing the company of Gypsy children of my age group. May and I, when we found the time, would get on our bikes and go Gypsy hunting. We knew all the stopping places locally and would do the rounds. Once we found a camp, the residents would tell us where other Gypsies were stopping and we kept in touch with most of those passing through the Mansfield and Sutton area. We could of course, visit the Gypsies down Carsic Lane, but found we were shunned by some of them due to Dad's drinking habits.

* * * * *

One consequence of Father's boozing was that we were poor to say the least. Coal, for instance, was about five shillings a hundredweight, but, more often than not, we could not afford to buy any and resorted to scavenging it where we could.

Next to our stopping place down Grove Road was the allotment of an old man called George Oliver. George's constant companion was a big, black, Labrador dog that answered to the name of Jet.

Sitting shivering in our trailer one night, without the means to make a fire, I was elected to chore (steal) some wongo (coal) from George's greenhouse bunker. Kneeling beside the shovel hole, filling a shopping bag, I heard a noise. George was coming to stoke his boiler. With nowhere else to go without being seen, I squeezed through the small, square shovel hole into the bunker, taking my shopping bag with me. Crouching at the back of the bunker and praying I wouldn't be caught, I nearly screamed when Jet's head came poking through the hole.

"Come out ert way yer daft owd bugger," George ordered. Jet had a good sniff at my legs before withdrawing his head. The shovel came almost to my feet as I made myself as small as I could in a corner of the bunker. Having stoked his boiler, George locked up and left, with Jet trailing behind. When all was quiet, I crept out of the bunker with my coal and hurried home. "I wouldn't do that again for love nor money," I told Mam.

I had resorted to using an old 'pram to collect rags and woollens. I'd take my hawking basket with me and do a bit of selling at the same time. When I had as many rags and woollens as I could manage, I'd weigh them in at one of the local scrap yards, either Old Ria Heath's in Mansfield, or more likely, Albert Caunt's in Sutton. David, then about three years old loved to go with me to weigh in at Albert's.

"Hello Mister Cunt," he would shout, as I arrived with my pram.

"Hello! You cheeky little devil," Albert would reply with a grin. Albert never failed to give little David half-a-crown, (twelve and a half pence) and on the way home I would stop and get David sweets with some of the money.

Some of the characters living in and around Grove Road afforded us much amusement, as I'm sure we did them. One couple in particular would have the whole family in fits of laughter with their antics. They were newlyweds and living with his mother in one of the small terraced houses at the end of Grove Road. Every Saturday night they would pass our trailers on their way to the Mason's Arms - the pub at the other end of the road and known locally as The Devil's Elbow. Looking very smart, they would walk past with the young lady clutching a small leather handbag. A couple of hours later the lass would be on her way back, going at a fair rate of knots with her husband in hot pursuit. She would be holding on to her hat and clutching the handbag tightly to her breast. Hubby would be bringing up the rear, a little under the weather and weaving from side to side, shouting.

"Give me that bloody bag. You don't think that ten bob is enough to have a decent drink do you? Give me that bloody bag you silly woman." But the silly woman was having none of it, and as she reached the house door, it would be flung open and she would disappear inside. His old mother would then appear at the door and with arms folded, would deny him access until he had calmed down and apologised to them both. This performance was enacted with slight variations most Saturday nights and we looked forward to it with keen anticipation.

Another character was Chick, a slow-witted man of around forty who was wont to call at our trailer on occasion.

"Can I look in your scrap for some nuts an' bolts an' that missis?" He would ask. Mother never turned him away despite we children being a little afraid of him.

"He won't 'urt you, he's only a poor dinglo," she would say.

Mother was washing one day and Chick was rooting around in Dad's scrap, when Chick said, "Have you got a bag missis?"

"Here," Mother said, throwing Chick a bag that had been covering the trailer tow bar, "Will that do?"

Chick grabbed the bag and threw it away in disgust, saying, "Not a f---ing bag missis, a f---ing bag."

We were about to drive him away when Chick put his fingers to his lips and made a smoking gesture.

"He wants a fag," Mother said, and our anger dissolved into laughter.

'Poor dinglo Chick,' we used to say, taking pity on the backward man. Maybe not as dinglo as we had thought. Weighing in at Albert Caunt's scrap yard one day, I saw Chick selling his scrap - a barrow full of nuts and bolts etcetera, collected no doubt from around our trailer.

Walking home from Sutton, down a particular street, a wary eye had to be kept open for Billy, another dinglo. Billy had a habit of lurking down one of the many passages between the houses and leaping out at unwary passers by, screeching like a stuck pig. He frightened the life out of Mother and I when he took us by surprise one evening. We had the last laugh however, in fact, we were doubled up with laughter when Billy's mother came out with a broom and chased him down the street.

"I'll teach you to frighten people, you bloody nincompoop," she called. Billy was crying as his mother chased him round the corner. I think it was the word nincompoop that made us laugh, more than the actions of the pair. Everyone knew Billy, and avoided him whenever possible.

Across the road from us was a small yard where my Grannie Florrie lived. Also living in this yard was an old Gypsy man by the name of Fred Holmes, who, through some sort of accident in his youth, was crippled. Fred lived with his sister Rowena, a tiny, beady-eyed woman who walked with the aid of a stick. Her standard mode of dress was a fur coat that had seen better days and a trilby hat with the brim turned up at the front.

"I bet that coat's as old as her," Dad remarked one day. "I'm sure it's got mange. I've never seen her without that hat and coat, she must go to bed in 'em." We children feared we might catch something from the coat and would never stand near Old Rowena.

Rowena's stick had other uses apart from its use as a walking aid. Many are the bucket of coal that has been neatly lifted over some garden wall, to disappear into her cavernous shopping bag. No item that lent itself to being hooked by a walking stick handle was safe when Rowena was about.

Early one morning, Dad sent me across to Old Fred's to beg a bit of firewood in order to make a fire in the trailer stove.

"Come on up my wench," Rowena called, when I shouted at the waggon steps. Climbing the steps and opening the door, I had difficulty hiding my amusement. There sitting up in bed, sipping a cup of tea was Rowena, complete with trilby hat and fur coat.

I was now in senior school and had lots of gaujo friends there. We would all meet up after school and perhaps go swimming at the local public baths. Evenings would find us in the milk bars, or maybe the pictures with our respective boy friends. My boy friend at the time was a good-looking Ukrainian called Eric. Saturday evenings were usually spent at the dance held at St. Michael's Church Hall, where we would meet up with many of the young Gypsies stopping in the locality.

One Sunday morning, my sister Geraline and I were walking to The Lawn when we saw two young Gypsy girls walking towards us. We stopped to talk and discovered they were sisters, Louie and Ann Lock.

"Where are you stoppin' at?" I asked.

"We're on Skegby Sands," Louie told us. "We've been there a week. Where are you goin'?"

"We were going to The Lawn," I said. "That's the park down the lane. But it doesn't

68

matter, we can go back to our place if you want, we're only stopping round the corner."

Louie and Ann came back with us to our trailer and I got on very well with them, Louie in particular. Their father it turned out, was full cousin to my mother.

I quite missed them when they moved, but a couple of months later I heard they were again on Skegby Sands.

May and I would often visit their camp, joining in a game of football perhaps with Louie, her brother Peter and their cousin Tom McCready. I didn't take much notice of Tom at the time, he seemed much older than the rest of us, two or three years at least. Other times we would sit in one of the waggons, talking or listening to records played on an old wind up gramophone salvaged from the scrap yard. Slim Whitman, Lonnie Donnegan and Hank Williams were our favourites.

Any time they were in the vicinity of our trailer, Louie's mother Lina and Tom's mother Annie would call for a chat with Mam. They would probably be on their way to Goodwin's, the tinsmith who made water jacks for the Gypsy community, or perhaps to the printers just a few hundred yards away.
Gypsy friends calling at one or other of these businesses frequently dropped in for a cup of tea and a natter, exchanging news of mutual friends and relatives elsewhere.

During the Christmas of 1954, Louie, who I hadn't seen for some months, called at our trailer.

"Where are you stopping? I asked. This is one of the first questions a Gypsy asks of another when they see each other.

"We're on a place called Mansfield Brickyard," Louie told me. "I can't stop long, I'm just on my way to pick some bills up from the printer's and I have to get back. Why don't you come over tomorrow afternoon? We can all go to the pictures or down the town or something."

"Alright, I will," I replied. "I'll be there about three and we'll decide what we're going to do."

Next day, I walked the two miles or so to Mansfield Brickyard and on arrival found that the pictures had already been decided upon. Several of us went, including Tom, who I liked right away once we got talking.

'He's not that much older than me,' I thought.

Coming out of the pictures later that day, Tom said, "It's very dark for you to walk all that way home on your own Julie. I'll walk back with you. Are you coming Louie?"

With Louie acting as chaperon, Tom walked me home with his arm around my waist.

Tom and I saw much more of each other after this. Usually we'd be with a group of young Gypsies, visiting cinemas, skating rinks, (roller of course) other Gypsies or just meeting up to talk and listen to records.

Walking home from a visit to Tom's one day, Louie decided to accompany me. We had to pass Mansfield reservoir on the way and Louie suggested we walked round it to watch the little sailing boats tacking to and fro across the water. Part way round we chanced to meet my old boy friend, Eric. He was riding the new racing 'bike his parents had bought him for Christmas.

"Hello Julie," he said. "I haven't seen you for a while. Your May tells me you've got a new boy-friend."

"She has," Louie retorted before I could speak. "What about it?"

Ignoring her, Eric turned to me and said, "Here, push my 'bike a bit."

"I can't be bothered with it," I said. "Push it yourself."

"Push it I said," Eric insisted. So, I pushed it - into the reservoir. Louie and I ran off laughing, leaving Eric to fish his 'bike out. That was the end of that friendship.

Not long after that Christmas, the Locks and McCreadys moved away. It didn't really bother me too much as Tom and I were not courting seriously and sister May and I started visiting Charlie and Louie Gaskin on Skegby Sands. They had a large family and Rosie, their eldest daughter was May's friend and I was friendly with Louie and Lena Gaskin. Boy friends were not on the agenda.

Mam and Dad were constantly at loggerheads and rows were a daily occurrence. After one particularly violent row, Dad left, going to stay with his brother George. He was away a couple of weeks, returning with a lorry he'd traded a car for. He seemed to have turned over a new leaf and settled down to work scrap dealing. May, now sixteen, went with him each day whilst Geraline, Dennis and I were packed off to school again. Mother, now pregnant again would go hawking each day, taking the youngest child, David, with her.

Christmas came and Dad started drinking again. Inevitably, rows and arguments followed in the same old familiar pattern. During one such row, Mother received a sever beating and had to be rushed into hospital to be delivered of my sister Teresa (known as Star) by emergency caesarian section.

I always intervened between Mam and Dad when the got violent and usually copped a punch or two. May, on the other hand, wouldn't have budged from her bed whatever the consequences. Many times, Mother, baby and I would be thrown out of the trailer, to spend the night wherever we could whilst Dad would usually adjourn to his mother's for the night. Here he would spend the night telling his mother how hard done by he was and keeping a watchful eye on our trailer to ensure we didn't return.

One such occasion arose when I got home about nine one evening from a visit to Tom's family who were stopping at Eastwood.

"Don't get your harness off when you sutto te-rarti," (sleep tonight) Mother warned. Meaning keep your clothes on when you go to bed tonight. ""He's got a bad do on 'im. There's goin' to be trouble when the pubs turn out. I think we'll be looking for somewhere to sleep tonight."

Sure enough, when we heard Dad coming down the lane he was shouting and cursing at the top of his voice and casting doubt on the parentage of all and sundry. Ripping the trailer door open, he immediately began attacking Mam. I couldn't just lie there and let it happen, so leaping out of bed, I went to Mam's defence.

As usual, Mother, baby Star and I ended up being thrown out for the night. Star's 'pram was always left outside with a sheet thrown over it to keep it dry, so with Star snuggled up as warm as we could make her in the 'pram we made our way down Sheepwash Lane to where The New Site had been.

Fortunately, the night was dry but it was bitterly cold. We settled down beneath some trees and made ourselves comfortable as best we could. After a while, Mother said. "I'm worried about the baby in this cold Julie. You'll 'ave to see if you can climb that tree an' chuck a bit of that dead wood down. We'll make a bit of a yog (fire) and keep us all warm. Go on, there's a good gel."

Having climbed the tree and broken off a fair amount of rotten limbs, I was halfway down when I was startled by the most fearful noise - something between a scream and a groan. When I'd gathered my wits a little, I tried to scramble down as fast as I could, but in my haste, missed my footing and fell to the ground with a thud, landing on my back. I was completely winded. I just couldn't move or speak. Mother was bending over me, trying to help me up when the noise came again.

"They do say this place is 'aunted," she said. "Maybe it's the Mullo."

Slowly, I got my breath back and was relieved to find I wasn't seriously hurt, just a few bruises and a bit of a headache.

We gathered the firewood together and soon had a good blaze going, but the noise came intermittently for the next hour or so. 'I'll not be sleeping tonight,' I thought, as I curled up by the fire. Nevertheless, I awoke to a bright frosty morning to find Mother stoking the fire with the last of the wood.

It didn't take long to find the cause of the unholy row in the light of day. Not fifty yards from our fire, a cow had given birth and the spindly-legged calf was doddering around, greedily taking its first milk. I for one was pleased to discover the noise had such an innocent explanation.

Making sure the fire was well and truly out, we made our way back to the trailer where I knew Mother would make Dad's life sheer hell for the rest of the day. Mother always had the upper hand when Dad was sober. And so the rows continued.

May was courting Dolphus Gaskin (Doodles) around this time. Doodles was stopping down Carsic Lane with his waggon and horses. I started seeing his brother, Ben. This courtship was short-lived however. I didn't like Ben's attitude so I stopped seeing him and my companions for the next few months were my gaujo girl friends.

Tom was back in the area again and on my way to meet some of my gaujo friends at the Kings cinema, I ran into him and his cousin Peter. We stood talking for a while and Tom told me he and Peter were on their way to the fair. "Why don't you come with us?" he asked. "You can see the picture at the Kings another time."

"Might as well," I replied nonchalantly. "I've seen it anyhow," I lied.

We enjoyed the fair and each other's company, and as we parted, Tom asked me to be his steady girl friend. I agreed.

From then on, we saw each other whenever we could. When Tom moved too far away for regular meetings,, he would phone me each evening. My nearest telephone kiosk was at the top of Grove Road and I would be there on the dot waiting for it to ring. Often we talked for ages, sometimes for an hour or more. Often the operator seemed to forget us and not request payment for further time. Our friendship became serious now and when apart we missed each other very much.

Arguments at home continued unabated. After one particularly bad beating, I ran away from home to stay with Tom's family. I was made very welcome but didn't realise at the time the pressure I must have put on both sets of patents. Staying with Tom's family in the Potteries, I received a letter from Dad threatening that he would go to the police if I weren't home by the weekend. I returned to the constant bickering and arguing.

*   *   *   *

Around August 1955, May ran away with Doodles, and Dad sent me to look for them.

"When you find 'em, tell her to come and fetch her belongings," he said.

After searching all the regular stopping places, I eventually found them camped with Doodle's father, Old Dozza Gaskin, at Forrest Town. I was not made very welcome to say the least, so I said my piece and went on my way.

I missed May when she went, although if she and Doodles were stopping anywhere near Sutton, we would often meet for a days hawking together.

May was seventeen when she left home and on her eighteenth birthday, she gave birth to her daughter Maria. Discharged from hospital, she would come to our place each morning carrying the baby in a sling, and go hawking with either Mother or me.

When they moved to Bilsthorpe, several miles away, May had to catch two 'buses to get to Grove Road. It was all a bit too much for her being newly confined so mother suggested that May leave her baby with me during the day.

Julie can look after the tikno (baby)," Mother said. "Someone's got to be in to look after Star an' David, so Julie might as well have Maria as well." My pay for looking after this bunch of terrors was two shillings a day, just enough for five Woodbines and 'busfare to see Tom.

May arrived to go hawking one morning with the news that she and Doodles were moving at the weekend. Somewhere in Lincolnshire, she said. It was to be two or three months before I saw her again.

I was at home with the two youngest children when she came, carrying baby Maria in her arms. When I saw May's face, I was taken aback. Her eyes were red and swollen from crying and she was obviously very distressed. I could have cried at the sight of her. Putting the baby on the bed, I started to make some tea.

"Whatever's happened May?" I asked. "What's happened to you?"

"It's him, Doodles," May said. "We had a row." She didn't elaborate further, and I thought it prudent not to press her.

Mother was heartbroken when she came home and saw May, and Dad was furious, vowing never to let May to go back to Doodles again. When May had recovered a little from the trauma, Dad took her out old stuffing with him. They worked hard and Dad bought another trailer to ease the overcrowding in the one we had. After a while, May wanted a waggon of her own. Dad found her one and repaired and re-painted it for her.

Months passed, and came the day when Doodles came looking for May. Dad and Doodles had a right old set to, all hell was let loose.

"And why aren't you married then?" Dad asked, in the heat of the argument. "If you wus any sort of a man you'd have married her. Perhaps you're married already. Is that it? Anyhow she doesn't come back unless she is married, and that's that."

The outcome was that May and Doodles did marry and stopped with us for some time after. May, unhappy with Doodles' drinking too much with Dad, eventually persuaded Doodles to move. They were getting on all right together when they left and live in harmony to this day.

I so looked forward to the evenings when I could get away and be with Tom. Often, Mother would be awkward and insist that I took David and Star with me. Unable to get the 'pram and two kids on the 'bus, I had arranged with Tom that should I not turn up as expected, he would catch the next 'bus back to our meeting place near the reservoir across from Kings Mill Hospital. On these occasions, we would go for a walk, or to a little cafe we knew for a snack. We were seen with the two children in tow so often that people used to think they were ours.

Whatever obstacles were put in our path we managed to overcome them and enjoy each other's company.

Tom's family had a lorry, which Tom drove, his Dad being unable to drive. Tom was rarely allowed to use it for pleasure however, so catching 'buses was the norm for us. When they were stopping at Jacksdale, we found it very convenient. The B7 bus from Sutton went right past the camp and there was a stop almost by the gate. I loved to go there and chat to the other Gypsy lads and lasses.

Louie and Peter Lock, Jimmy Finney, two or three of Charlie Gaskin's children and Tom and I would go around together. We'd go roller skating, swimming or perhaps to the cinema. Other times would find us listening to records or having a singsong in Tom's parent's tent. A happy go lucky crowd of youngsters. But Tom and I knew we would marry some day, when I was a little older.

Time wouldn't pass quickly enough for Tom and me, we were keen to marry as soon as we could. We'd make plans and dream about living together, not giving much thought as to where the money would come from to provide somewhere to live once wed. When May left with Doodles, I assumed I would take her place working with Dad. It was not to be however, Dad would always find himself a partner to work with from somewhere.

Star must have been about ten or eleven months old when Mam and Dad had their most viscous row. So violent was the fight, Mother was taken to Mansfield General Hospital where she received some fifty stitches to wounds about her head and body. Dad threatened me and I was very frightened - he seemed totally unaware of the fact that he had almost killed my Mam. Taking Star and Brother David with me, I made my way to Eastwood, near Nottingham, where Tom was staying. Worried about Mother I went home next day to find that Dad had been taken into custody and Mother had signed herself out of hospital.

At Dad's trial, Mother refused to press charges but the police charged him with causing grievous bodily harm and he was sent to prison. Whilst Dad was inside, I went hawking to help keep the family. Sometimes I would meet up with Tom and his parents as they were going about their business and they would give me a lift to some fresh hawking.

Jimmy Finney was staying with Tom's family whilst they were in the Jacksdale and Eastwood area. He was fond of Louie Lock but she didn't seem to take him seriously despite the many presents he bought her.

"We're moving to the Potteries on Sunday," Tom announced one evening. I was saddened to hear this news, but we promised to keep in touch by phone and letter. Sunday came all too soon and he was gone. We kept in touch as we had promised and the weeks went by.

Telephoning one evening, Tom surprised me with the news that he and Jimmy were coming to visit by train, and asked if I would tell Louie and would we both meet them in a cafe in Mansfield.

Louie was still at Jacksdale and I went to visit her there. We arranged that she would call for me on the Sunday of Tom and Jimmy's visit on the pretext that we were going swimming together. "Louie's calling for me at eleven Mam," I told her that Sunday morning. "We're going to Sutton baths for a swim."

"Your not going swimming in this weather," Mother retorted. "It's freezing out there wench. You'll catch yer death of cold. Whatever are you thinking of." To be honest, it was cold with a dusting of snow on the ground.

"But we'll be alright Mam," I begged. There's hair dryers and everything at the baths and we can have a cup of tea in the cafeteria and be bone dry before we come out. Go on, let us go. Louie's coming all the way from Jacksdale to go with me." Just then Louie turned up to add her pleas to mine and reluctantly, Mother relented and of we went. Hiding our bags containing our swimming stuff in a hedge bottom, Louie and I walked to Mansfield in time to meet the lads at eleven thirty.

We spent the day in Mansfield and walking round Sutton reservoir before Tom and Jim decided we should all go back to Louie's place at Jacksdale. With almost an hour to wait for a 'bus we went to a little cafe in Sutton for a snack. Jimmy ordered egg and chips and was carrying his meal to the table when the egg slid off his plate and onto the floor. We all fell about laughing when he picked the egg up, blew on it and put it back on his plate. "You've got to eat so much muck before you die," he laughed. Sitting down, he proceeded to eat up with relish, much to the disgust of a rather snooty lady at the next table.

Waiting for the 'bus, Jimmy and Louie had a row and by the time the 'bus came, they weren't on speaking terms. Now Jimmy almost always carried a guitar with him and today was no exception - it was strapped across his back as usual. On the 'bus Jimmy started to play, and improvised a song about his coming all the way from the Potteries just to have a row. It was hilarious and when he'd finished, the other passengers clapped, whistled and shouted for more, but Louie was not to be won over with his serenading, and there their courtship ended.

During the summer of '56, the gaujos living within earshot of my parent's rows got up a petition to have us moved. An eviction notice was issued by the local council giving a date by which we should move and threatening court action should we refuse to go. Consequently, we moved to Shirebrook, in Derbyshire, where we were joined a few days later by May and Doodles.

May, Mother and I would go hawking together, taking Star and baby Maria with us. Geraline was left to look after things at home and the other kids were sent to school.

Meeting Tom was more difficult from Shirebrook and involved catching two 'buses, but we managed. Sometimes, Tom would catch a 'bus to Mansfield and I would meet him there. We were very keen to get married by now and were trying to pluck up courage to ask for my parent's consent. Should consent not be forthcoming, we planned to run away to Gretna Green.

Dad decided we had to move from Shirebrook. I'm not sure why but he and Doodles spent a couple of days looking for another stopping place, without success.

Dad's lorry didn't have a towbar fitted and we had two trailers to move plus Doodles' waggon. I suggested we might move to Jacksdale where Tom was stopping and eventually this course of action was agreed, much to my delight. Tom came and moved our two trailers and Doodles moved his waggon. I don't remember if he had a horse of his own or if he borrowed one.

Jacksdale was a muddy camp to say the least but I was pleased to be near Tom and amongst so many other Gypsies. Stopping there were Gaskins, Vareys, Braddocks, Ayres', Finneys, Tom's Uncle Sam and Aunt Lina Lock plus many other whose name I can't recall.

Tom worked with Dad and Doodles for a while but I don't think he approved of their habit of calling in the pub as soon as it opened, so that partnership was soon dissolved. I continued to hawk with my mother and sister May. Mother got on quite well with Tom's mother and with his aunts, Louie and Lina. The foursome would often go to the pictures together of an evening. Many small villages boasted a cinema in those days and Jacksdale was no exception. It was only a short walk from our camp and the programme changed three times a week.

Tom and I often talked of getting married but you had to be twenty one to marry without parental consent in those days and I was much younger. Nevertheless we walked to Selston Church one Sunday and spoke to the Reverend Pearce, who told us that the banns had to be read out in church on three consecutive Sundays. The earliest date we could marry, he said, would be October 21st. and this date was agreed. Giving us a form of consent to be signed by my parents, he also arranged that we go to the vicarage one evening to have the wedding service explained and to satisfy him that we knew what we were doing.

"You'll have to ask Mam and Dad by yourself," I told Tom. "I'm too trashed

"I'm trashed myself," said Tom. "But it's got to be done."

When Tom approached my parents, I kept out of the way and waited anxiously in his mother's tent.

"They've signed, they've signed," he said, when he found me, waving the bit of paper and grinning all over his face. Delighted, we took the precious form with us to vicarage when we went for our prearranged interview.

Clothes for the wedding were our next concern, neither of us having any good clothes to wear. We went to Burton's in Mansfield to order them. I ordered a two piece suit, or costume as we called it. Tom had a suit made Gypsy fashion, with gauntlet cuffs, open seams and patch pockets. Double breasted, it had pleats and a half belt in the back of the coat. My costume was air-force blue, with three quarter length coat and a skirt with three box pleats back and front. Both outfits came to about twenty pound and we paid a deposit with the balance payable on collection.

Hawking every day with my mother, I gave her most of what I earned but kept a little back each day towards paying for the clothes. Whilst hawking, Mother begged me a new, half-moon feathered hat, blue to match my costume. I bought a pink and blue blouse and a pair of black suede shoes. Tom's suit was navy blue and he bought a pale blue shirt and a navy blue tie. His shoes were brown.

Tom's mother and I went to buy the ring. We found one in a pawnshop in Sutton. A man's ring, it was much too big but at the princely sum of eight pounds was as much as we could afford. We left it to be sized and arranged to pick it up at the weekend.

Most of the Gypsies left Jacksdale over the next week or two, leaving just my family, Tom's family and May and Doodles in resident. This didn't bother me, I was so excited at the thought of being married at last. Tom visited his Aunt Lina, Charlie Gaskin and the others stopping in the lane at Derby to invite them all to the wedding but no one came. On the big day, there was just our parents and Doodles and May.

Carnations for buttonholes had been ordered, one pink for me and white for everyone else. On our way to collect them, we called at Woolworth's in Sutton to buy Tom some socks. The Manageress was just opening the doors when we arrived.

"You're an early bird me duck," she said to Tom as he followed her in.

"I'm getting married in a couple of hours," Tom told her. "And I need a pair of socks."

When Tom came to pay for the socks, he was told, "Have them on me, and I wish you good luck and every happiness." Although the socks turned out to be our only wedding present, it didn't bother us, we had each other.

Tom's lorry was our transport for the wedding with Doodles doubling as chauffeur and best man. He dropped Tom and his parents at the church first, returning to collect my parents, May and a very nervous bride to be.

The church seemed cavernous and quiet with just the eight of us there and I was glad when the ceremony was over. After the wedding, we retired to the Butcher's Arms for an impromptu reception.

We began our married life living in a tent borrowed from Tom's parents. All we owned was a pair of new sheets I had bought a few weeks previous, a chrome biscuit barrel I'd begged whilst hawking, the clothes we were married in and about eight pounds in cash. Nevertheless, we were together and very happy.

Despite predictions that it would never last - I was much too young it was said - at the time of writing this, Tom and I have been married forty years. We've had our ups and downs, joys and woes, and raised five kids of whom I'm very proud in the process. We've had a full, and in the main, happy life together.

But that, as they say, is another story.

Glossary of Traveller Words

Boshni - pheasant
Dinglo - stupid, a fool
Gaujo - non-Gypsy
Grasni - mare
Hochiwichi - hedgehog
Kek - no
Kitchimer - pub
Kushti - good
Mullo - devil
Old stuffing - See Tatting
Puvin greis - grazing of horses
Rumied - married
Spivying - painting farm barns
Trash - frighten
Wongo - coal

Chore - steal
Drabengro - doctor
Gavo - hide
Grie - horse
Jukle - dog
Kanengro - hare
Kory - penis
Livner - beer
Muskeros - police
Puv - field
Romanies - Gypsy words
Shushi - rabbit
Tatting - collecting rags, scrap metal etc
Tuvlo - cigarette
Yog - fire

Indices

Moss 55
Newberry 55, 61
Oliver 66
Price 36, 37, 41, 55, 61
Rook 55
Rowles 3
Smith 36, 37, 61
Stevenson 28
Sykes 3
Taylor 4, 41, 50, 55, 61
Teaton 8, 26
Toogood 8, 21
Varey 3, 6, 8, 11, 17, 22, 28, 31, 34,
          36, 38, 39, 41, 43, 45, 47
Walton 11, 55
Winter 3, 20, 55, 64, 65
Woodward 55, 61
Wooley 60

Places

Allestree 41
Alsager 3
Appleby 57
Barnaby Dun 57
Barnsley 36, 37, 60, 63
Belfast 33, 35
Bilsthorpe 23, 35, 72
Black Country 17
Boroughbridge 52
Bourne 50
Brough 57
Bulwell 28, 39, 43
Buxton 22
Cannock Chase 31
Cheadle 18, 22, 30, 42
Cheshire 11
Chesterfield 21, 34, 35
Chesterton 6, 18, 27, 31, 32
Congleton 11
Crewe 8
Derby 17, 22, 41, 48

Derbyshire 11, 39
Dinnington 30, 39
Dublin 4
Dunkirk 17
Eastwood 42, 70, 73
Eckington 41
Forest Town 72
Grantham 39

Gretna Green 74
Halmer End 3, 7
Hazel Grove 3
Heaton Norris 2
Hilton 59
Ireland 3
Jacksdale 41, 45, 47, 73, 74, 75
Lancashire 11
Leek 22
Lee Gap 52
Lincolnshire 39, 51, 58, 72
Liverpool 33
London 22
Longport 29
Manchester 7, 38
Mansfield 28, 34, 36, 39, 41, 61, 65,
          66, 67, 69, 73, 74
Newcastle under Lyme 10, 18
Northern Ireland 33
Nottingham 33
Nottinghamshire 11, 39
Pilsley 63
Potteries 3, 28, 42, 44, 71, 73
Ripley 41
Rotherham 37
Royston 37, 38
Sandiacre 27, 29
Selston 47, 75
Sheffield 30
Shirebrook 44, 74
Singapore 3
Skegby 33, 36, 40, 44
South Yorkshire 11
Staffordshire 11
Stairfoot 36, 37, 60, 63
Staveley 41

78

General Index

80